Tales to Tell

Tales to Tell

Memoir

Tracy G. Herrick

To order additional copies of this book, contact:
Xlibris Corporation
1-888-795-4274
www.Xlibris.com
Orders@Xlibris.com
102170

To Maie,
with gratitude and love

Maie, Sylvi Anne, Matthias Niklaus,
Noora Pearl, and Siena Jade to carry on

Table of Contents

Foreword

I am writing this really for members of my family who have yet to be born and who someday may wonder who one of their ancestors was when he walked on the earth—what he was like, what he did, and what his thoughts were about.

I will never know these family members to be, but I want them to know that they come from a fine lineage which they can be proud of. They have my hopes for their happiness and a fulfilling and long life, as mine has been.

Preface

Tracy and I met at age five in kindergarten at Lincoln Elementary, Lakewood, Ohio. I have only dim recollections of that first school year. I have no memory of any time that we have not been friends. Now seventy-three years later, Tracy asked me to pen a few words for this preface. His memoir will be recognized by all who know him as pure Herrick—brief paragraphs, short sentences swept clean of extra words, and cumbersome vocabulary. I should add that he was famous for lists of three (e.g., three reasons for this or that, three consequences of something, etc.).

Tracy the man—there is so much to say. May I begin by noting his brevity in expression, written and verbal, expressed with humility and without calling attention to defects in character or actions present and past of anyone historical or living. His humility belies a broad liberal education (in the classical sense) and great intellect. His humility is neither studied nor a disguise, but an exceptional gift given careful instruction from family and school, carefully honed and revered by friends and acquaintances, associates, and family.

Civility: This is a true element in the true character of the man—absolutely civil in demeanor and actions, considerate of others, kind in thought and utterance, and, of course, with minimum words. Tracy is a skilled conversationalist, an adept communicator.

Humor: In my memory to this day are many examples of Tracy (a.k.a. Mr. Good Humor, and, sometimes, Mr. Clown). I think it started with vinyl records of Spike Jones and Victor Borge. We imitated Borge's audible punctuation amid gales of laughter.

One such occasion was followed by a lesson about fugues at an upright piano, illustrating different voices in a Bach fugue. All this probably at age maybe nine or ten.

Tracy's humor continued with little acts like halting a piano recitation at high school to fish an oil can from inside the piano to lubricate, with great flair and audible clicks, a squeaky piano stool . . . straight from Borge. The student body just howled. Later, he skillfully acted the part of the professor in Thornton Wilder's play *Our Town*, then a popular high school production.

Till now he has maintained his humor through the trials of time, as well as his lifelong interest and skill at the keyboard. The latest? A plan to promote small benefit recitals by prominent musicians and pianists in St. Augustine, Florida, with a swimming pool between artist and audience to get the audible dimension of sound reflecting from water.

Tracy is trying to corner the market on used Steinway pianos. There is a beautiful antique walnut Steinway fully restored with modern action in their Palo Alto home, another Steinway at their Pine Mountain Lake getaway, a third in the home of their daughter and son-in-law, and a fourth will no doubt magically appear in their new Florida cottage now under construction in St. Augustine near family and grandchildren.

A self-indulgence, perhaps, but truly a love of music and the pure sound from the finest of instruments.

Tracy's economic interests were probably awakened by his grandfather Herrick, who was a vice-president at Cleveland Trust Bank (later Bank One). Then he learned at a young age the magic of compounding *interest*, and importantly, that economics is really about matters of society, its health, energy, monies—its value, distribution and allocation.

It took reviewing his memoir, page by page, to part his veil of humility and reveal some of Tracy's professional achievements. That he penned several books, one of which went into 8 editions and is still read, that he invented a monthly economic newsletter, *The Money Analyst*, and never missed a deadline in over 25 years, and that he served with distinction as an outside member on the Board of Directors of the Jefferies & Co. for over 16 years, are all marks of the professional man.

Throughout his distinguish career, Tracy has received many

awards and special notice from peers, publishers, the *Wall Street Journal* and organizations for achievements in economics and skill forecasting economic conditions. Today, in retirement, many seek his comments and analysis of economic news.

It is a privilege to know and be a friend of this remarkable man and his wife, Maie. Thank you Tracy for the opportunity to put these thoughts into a Preface to your memoir.

Claude Rust, PhD
August 30, 2011

Introduction

I have been unaccountably lucky.

I mean lucky in the big sense of the word, such as standing at Forty-first Street and Fifth Avenue in New York City, then stepping back to get out of the wind and rain on a blustery March day; and where I had been standing moments before, a brick fell from the building, smashing to smithereens against the concrete sidewalk.

It was a transitory moment for me. I was alive and completely safe. I could have been snuffed out. There seems to be no explanation of how that could have happened. This sort of occurrence has happened again and again.

My luck holds in other more complex ways. Often it occurs as an initial difficulty, which turns out to protect me in a way I had not realized would be important. Sometimes it involves meeting exactly the right person at the right time.

I have never forgotten that virtually all of the people around me are as intelligent as I am, or are more so. I have done nothing that they could not have done as well or better.

This is not a disadvantage in any way.

They are usually too far ahead of their friends and coworkers, and their potential contributions often fall on deaf ears. I am happy to say that has not been my experience.

I wonder why nothing important that I have ever planned has come to pass. In fact, all of my plans seem to have been useless. Rather, everything important has come as a surprise—a strike of lightning.

This has taken many forms. It includes the chance meeting of my wife of nearly a half of a century, the sudden loss of my son, the special recognition by the president of Estonia, and many other events that came out of the blue.

Strangely, in virtually all of these instances, I somehow knew in advance that they would happen.

Sometimes this knowledge would come in a dream and be as vivid and realistic as something that would occur in broad daylight. Other times, it would be a strong feeling that something would happen, and this feeling would recur again and again.

There is so much that I don't understand but has been crucial to my work and life.

I would not trade my life for anything. I would gladly live it over, even the tragic moments which have been painful beyond description. Each moment has been precious. I am grateful for all of these years.

Life is all we really have.

Chapter 1

Dawn

1933 to 1938

I was born into a family of four on December 30, 1933, at 2:36 p.m. at Lutheran Hospital in Cleveland, Ohio.

My father was Stanford Avery Herrick, and my mother was Elizabeth Grant Smith. They lived with my father's parents.

My parents lived this way, I was told, because my father could not make enough money for the three of us to live in our own home. The proof of this was the failed attempt to manage to live in a rented small house on Tiedeman Road when I was a one-month-old. The story went that my grandparents came over to visit and found no food on the premises. After that, my parents moved back to live with my grandparents.

Of course, this was 1934, in the depths of the business depression. Most people were simply without enough money for even basic necessities.

But this family of five resided also in a small house. There were many bosses. But I survived and apparently thrived. And what choice did I have?

My father was a gasoline station attendant. He put gasoline in the tank, checked the oil, and wiped the windows, as well as washed the headlights if there was time. And if there was more time, he also checked the air pressure in the tires. The list of services which were performed for the ordinary visit at a service station would amaze contemporary drivers. This type of work paid very little and held out little prospect for company advancement. He probably did not make enough money to be self-supporting.

My mother was from Kentucky, a state to the south of Lakewood, Ohio, where we lived. She always liked to play up her Southern background. This did not go over smoothly with my grandparents, who had strong Northern proclivities. But Mother had spunk and always kept an edge to everything.

My parents met when my mother attended a dance at Western Reserve University, which was the university that my father was attending. He began as a freshman in 1929 and most probably met her in 1932, when my father would have been a junior classman. He was not a scholar and had difficulty keeping up with his classes. Somehow they were married; he left the university and became a gasoline attendant.

My grandmother Blanche Herrick was crippled with rheumatoid arthritis and could barely walk. She was a kind lady, but with a rod of steel in her backbone. She gave an air of quiet nobility and always expected that I do my best. She was always good to me. I was like her second son. I suspect that her first boy, my father, was a bit of a disappointment to her. I am sure she did not relish the thought of a three-party family living in her house in what turned out to be years and years.

My grandfather, also named Tracy Herrick and for whom I was named, was paterfamilias. His middle name was Ellis, and mine is Grant. He ruled the house, and his domain extended to all whom could be called upon. He was always generous to me and gave me expensive gifts which he could not afford and which my friends could not believe. He was assistant vice president of the Cleveland Trust Company, which was the largest bank in the state.

So he had a steady income through all the years of the Depression. He stood out in every way from the ordinary dad. Everything had to be on a colossal scale, but it was always a big puff—nothing ever lasted. But what a dreamer! One time, he talked about running for governor, and it went on from there.

There was one other person in our immediate family, and that was Sally. This angel from heaven was the all-around helper in the household. She looked after everybody, and she did her tasks while singing a song. I know this very well, because as a three-year-old, I was always telling her, "No radio, Sally," meaning that she was a radio and should turn off her singing. Sally's optimism and good nature knew no end. She literally kept the family together. There were too many agendas for a small space; Sally kept us human and talking to one another.

I also had a dog. He was a toy terrier. I can't remember his name. I just assume he was a boy dog, but at age three or four, these matters don't take on much importance. I liked him very much, but he was not a pal as later dogs became.

My first remembrance of anything specific was lying in bed and hearing Mother's high heels striking the slate sidewalk as she was walking toward our house. It was a very piercing sound, almost echoing off our neighbor's house. The sound was emphatic. Something was not the way she wanted it to be, and she was sending out signals that she would have to be reckoned with. I remember feeling that I was involved. It was not a happy feeling.

And yet there was beauty in the rhythm of the steps. They came in a steady beat, with an occasional interruption as if she lost her balance from time to time. But for the most part, there was regularity. It was a kind of music.

It awoke me to the power of sound.

I spent most of my time with my mother. She took me with her wherever she went. We took many little trips. We went down the street; we went in stores since Mother loved to look at merchandise. But she never bought anything because she didn't have any money.

My father seemed overwhelming. He was six feet three inches. He could toss me way up in the air, and he would firmly catch me. He was always doing things a bit on the rough side. This was particularly true when he asked me to help him fix his car. Cars in those days always had something wrong with them. Car owners would pride themselves on their ability to fix cars.

Nothing was ever really fixed, but tolerances with everything were wide, and the repairs were within a zone of improvement. But there was often shouting. If the problem was something like a nut that would come loose, then there was swearing.

I felt intimidated by these sessions, and when they were approaching, I would try to slink away out of the line of fire. I didn't know what the words meant, but the tone of the words was critical. I think my dad wanted to impress me that it was all right to be tough. He wanted me to be able to protect myself and to be able to keep my friends safe in a world that he saw was often hostile. My reaction was to get away from tirades of any kind. I simply did not like them.

We had a telephone in our house. Most people had a phone by the late 1930s. But then one day, without any reason, it seemed, the phone was gone. The phone had been a link to the outside, and even though I did not speak on the phone on any kind of regular basis, it was still a precious link to the outside. When it left, I felt something important was missing. It was a bit like being isolated. I was troubled by the disappearance of the phone but never discussed it with anybody. That was the way it was supposed to be. A little boy had no business thinking about where a phone was. The telephone eventually reappeared. It was like magic. One day, it was gone; the next, it was returned. Its return came as a great relief to me. Nobody else cared about that.

One day, my grandfather unloaded some bags from the trunk of his car. Then another day, he unloaded more bags.

These were mixed with sand, and he laid a foundation about ten feet by fifteen feet. Nobody was allowed to step on this firmament until it was dry and secure. That seemed to be a long time. I wanted to see for myself what had been done. Then after a while, the floor began to crumble. From what I heard, this base was intended to be a floor for a new room, something like a sunroom.

But it was ruined because what was described as unclean sand was used. This sand must have come from a beach on Lake Erie. I know this must have been a great disappointment to my grandfather, but I never recalled that he showed that he was sad about the matter. He kept a high profile through it all. I remember that my feelings were never to build something that would crumble. The disappointment was too great. I didn't have this worked out in carefully arranged language. Rather, it was only a feeling, an impression. But it was real.

Mother would take me with her on her trips. She would always put on good clothes when we went out, and she would fuss over them so that they were just as she wanted them to be. She had a friend who lived on the next street in a house with three white pillars. Her friend also had a little person—a son or daughter—who was a nice playmate for me. Then one day, we stopped going over to this house.

I never understood why and was sad to lose my playmate. When we went downtown, Mother often took me with her. We would take the streetcar and get off at the Public Square. It was a short walk to the May Company, which was Mother's favorite store. I always liked to go to this store because they had a children's playroom. There were lots of things to play with that were not available elsewhere—I remember big blocks as one of these. It cost twenty-five cents per hour to play in that room. Sometimes Mother didn't have the extra twenty-five cents; I would sit on a chair and watch her shop, wishing I could be in the playroom.

Mother also took me to visit her sister, my aunt Jean, who had a son named John. Judy, a daughter, had not yet arrived. We played together, and I liked John. I remember that they lived in an apartment on the east side of town. They had a long hall in the apartment; and for some reason, I liked to place the dining room chairs in a row, like box cars in a train, and try to push them down the hall. My aunt Jean never liked this and made me stop it. I never knew what the trouble was.

The times that were most joyful were when Mother and Dad piled into their car and headed South to Mother's family in Danville, Kentucky. The trip took eight hours, which is a long time to bounce around the backseat of a car. But it was worth it. My parents were happy, surrounded by a fun-loving, prankster-prone group of several interrelated families. I was part of this gang of individuals. These people were farmers and knew hard work. But when we arrived, work was for another day. It was as if a cloud had lifted. I felt a part of this extended family and tried my little jokes to the glee of a receptive audience. I was as free as a little boy could be. I wished the time there would last forever.

I was completely protected from adversity. Or at least I have no recollection of family stress. Perhaps the most stressful event of this period of my life was the death of my grandfather's brother. The two of them grew up on a farm in Twinsburg, Ohio, which is located about forty miles southeast of Cleveland. Both went to work for banks in Cleveland; and my grandfather's brother, whose name was Avery, actually had risen rapidly to vice president of Central National Bank. I worked for that bank one summer, and many people in the bank remembered him and liked him. This death was stressful enough, but he died from carbon monoxide inhalation. The cause of this was never made quite clear, which must have added even more grief. I was three and a half and have no recollection of the event.

Perhaps the event that marked the end of this early time of my life was when I was six years old, going on seven, and Mother was lying on the sofa in Aunt Jean's apartment. She was obviously very sick, and for some reason, I had not seen her become ill. I was struck by her condition and wanted to know what the matter with her was. Nobody answered me. There was lots of talk about an operation. People would come and go. Some would say for her to have the operation; others would tell her not to have it. The scene was all very confusing. I listened, trying to figure it out. I remember that I felt she should not have the operation, even though it was obvious that she was not feeling well. I told her this, and she was irritated at that.

But it was more than that. Mother later spoke of this as a time when she had a cancer or a tumor. And maybe it was. But at a later time in Florida, Aunt Jean had a few too many drinks, took me aside, and said that Mother had been pregnant at this time and was feeling ill due to the pregnancy. The operation, which I remembered, was whether or not she should have an abortion, which I gather she did have. I could have had a brother or sister. But these were difficult times for Mother as well as my family. In fact, my family was about to come apart.

Chapter 2
Divorce
1939 to 1940

I had no real idea of what was going on, but something serious was wrong. There was a feeling of dislike among people who lived very close to one another. Nobody was talking.

Mother was the outsider. The other members of the family had become constantly critical of her. I didn't know exactly what people were saying, but I felt the tone.

There had been storms of words at earlier times, but this one was different. It ended with my mother and my father going separate ways. I was in the middle. Something was awry. Mother's operation, which she had, was different. I recall my father did not want her to have it.

But whatever the underlying issue was, the crisis arrived a day before Christmas Eve. Mother was by the front door, and she was holding some keys. My grandfather was in the living room, standing back away; my grandmother was seated in a chair near the front door, and my father was middistance. I had been upstairs in my room, heard the commotion, came to the stairs, and looked at a scene like the aftermath of a big fight. Mother said she was leaving for good. I had feared this moment for a long time. I could not believe it was happening, and I burst into tears and wailed.

I never had cried so hard in my life. I was transfixed and couldn't move from the stair I was on. I remember saying, "Don't go, Mother, don't go." She handed the keys—I presume to the house—to my grandmother, opened the door, and left. My life was now going to be very different. The extra joking and play in the house would be gone. There would be no foil to my father, and a heavy seriousness would prevail. But that was the future. That night, I cried myself to sleep.

I was almost seven years old—my birthday was a few days after this happened. I was in the second grade. I was living day to day, just keeping my head above water. In fact, it took five years for me to figure out what had happened and to get myself in shape to deal with things in a really satisfactory way. I failed many times. But I never doubted that I always had to pick myself up.

In any event, the immediate aftermath of all of that night's happening was to do things that would make it possible for my father to get custody of me. In those days, this was a nearly impossible task. Mothers invariably got custody of a child in a divorce.

My grandfather, who had studied law but did not practice, mapped out the strategy. There were two parts. First, the judge would need to be convinced that I should stay with my father. Judges decided these things. That involved, first, my indicating this to the judge and, second, making me into a model student and that this training would be maintained.

Here, my father stepped aside and let my grandfather do the talking. He did the job in full regalia. He described the opportunities that I would enjoy if I remained with my father— and grandfather—he described a way of growing up that was similar to most judges and one that they would be sympathetic toward. It was a life of good education, good introductions, and established people—all what my grandfather stood for. He contrasted this way of life with that of my mother, who was broke, without a family, and who could barely afford subsistence living. The reality of our situation was far less than my grandfather's image. But images count in law.

This meant that I should act and dress like a gentleman. I was to wear a tie every day to school. It meant that I should not do the ordinary things that boys do—no roughhouse, no hard-impact sports, better than that, no sports at all. I should show utmost courtesy to teachers and all prominent people. And most miraculous of all, I was to get a beautiful suit from Baker & Co., which was the best men's clothing company in the city of Cleveland.

All of this was preparatory to my meeting the judge personally. It was not usual—but also not unusual for a seven-year-old child to tell the judge in a divorce case which parent was preferred. This was done on a low-key basis in a meeting in the judge's chambers. My grandmother rehearsed me. She said I should tell the judge exactly what I would like to happen. She said I should tell the judge this was my own wish and that I was not repeating what someone else was telling me to say. Then she asked me to go over this and tell her what I planned to say.

She gave an even hand to her instructions. But of course, I knew the consequences of the meeting with the judge. And all of the good things that had been lavished on me, including my beautiful suit, were very much involved. I walked into the judge's chambers and was the model little boy of the time. I tried to show good manners everywhere. I told the judge I wanted to stay where I was; he smiled and left. It was all over in less than three minutes. I stayed with my father.

Throughout all of this, my grandfather read to me pages of the book *Little Lord Fauntleroy*, which is a book about a young nobleman who has a lot of good sense and helps the ordinary people in the village below to do their work better. I never liked the book but listened.

Mother lived with her sister, Aunt Jean, while she got her feet on the ground. She found a job as a girl Friday in the production planning department at Weatherhead & Company. The company manufactured parts fittings and valves for all kinds of machinery. It was Mother's job to keep the files in order and to find something when one of the people in the department wanted it. I heard people say she was good at her job. This didn't surprise me when I thought about it in later years. Mother had a very good mind when she applied it. But she never liked the job. In fact she never liked any job. It turned out that the work at Weatherhead was the only job she held throughout her entire life.

Once Mother got a job, she rented a room near Aunt Jean. Under the terms of the divorce agreement, I was allowed to visit Mother four hours each week on Sunday between two and six o'clock in the afternoon. So for a year, she entertained me in the home of Aunt Jean and in her small but neat room. She tried hard to make the time with her pleasant. She bought a spinet piano, which she took back after I said something about the piano having a tinny sound. That was clearly the wrong thing to say.

Aunt Jean kept up a barrage of pot shots against my father and grandfather and grandmother, which I felt was irritating. I simply wanted everybody to get along. I had enough hard knocks to last a long time.

There was one other person in my immediate family, my grandmother Smith, who I called Gramma Smith. She was my mother's mother. Her husband, who was my other grandfather, had left Gramma Smith in 1930 or thereabouts, and Gramma Smith left her home in Kentucky to get work in Cleveland as a seamstress. She brought her two girls in tow with her.

Gramma Smith was a quiet person. She seldom talked to me. I suspect she couldn't figure me out. I acted quite differently than the little boys in rural Kentucky. I was being developed into a model child of the dominant Northern commercial culture. Little boys on the farm lived a life a million miles away.

But Gramma Smith genuinely cared for me. As I grew older, she then sensed what I was about, and I felt her sympathetic hopes that I would find my place and be content. She was stability of a kind, and I liked that. But she was remote from my daily life, and she lived with Aunt Jean, who always seemed to speak for her. Yet as I will tell later, when I was seventeen, she did something that was utterly fantastic and could have changed my life.

Mother did not stay in this situation very long. Within a year, she married Barney McLaughlin, who was about fifteen years older than she. Barney worked in her department at Weatherhead; a nice man, a quiet man, whom I got along with pretty much. He could be a bit strong on his preferences for what I didn't like at the time. This included football games at the windswept stadium by the lake and some sausage that Mother made for him and I had to eat. But for the most part, Barney was okay.

My father, on the other hand, had the upper hand for my life. He could pretty well do and demand what he wanted from me. He didn't demand much, except when he got into a shouting session. He tried not to do this, and I felt this, but it would be as if something would come over him. I suspect that he didn't understand everything about himself in a fundamental way. Anyway, my grandmother would always protect me, and an hour later, everything would have blown over.

He gave me a model sailboat on the Easter following the divorce. I adored this boat. Most of all, I was thrilled when he took me to a small lake next to the art museum. There, I would carefully place my boat in the water, and always a breeze or gust of wind would set it off on a course to the other side of the lake. I would run around the lake to greet this boat. We would come here often at this time of my life. My father knew I liked to do this, and he wanted to make me happy; I never felt he was very much thrilled. But he tried to make my life upbeat in doing this.

Later that spring, father was stricken with appendicitis, and the appendix ruptured. This would be a serious matter in today's times. In 1941, it was life threatening. It started with a stomachache that kept getting worse. My father never liked to go to doctors. For one reason, he never liked to spend the money. Moreover, he was skeptical about their ability to do what needed to be done. So he kept away from medical help until he was sick, truly sick.

Following the operation, he was lying in the hospital bed when I visited him. He had tubes from his midsection. When I saw that, I suddenly became afraid. I was scared he would die. I felt something was terribly wrong. I wanted to hide. Then our visit was over. It was the scariest moment I ever spent in a hospital. My father recovered. He beat the odds.

My father would usually take me over to Mother for my allotted four hours a week with her. He would drive me in his black 1935 Ford Tudor with an overpowered V-8 engine and weak mechanical brakes. Even when it was brand new, it was an inherently unsafe car. But nobody worried about that.

When my father bought a motorcycle, that was a different

matter. A motorcycle ran against the grain of everybody. My grandmother did not want her son, who was from a so-called respectable family, to ride up to a friend's house on such a contraption. Grandfather had no friends who rode one, and Mother was afraid of an accident where I would fall off the back. But Father kept the machine, and I liked it. It was powerful and shook all over when it accelerated, and it could beat any car in a start-up from a traffic light. I was never injured from it in any way.

Grandmother did something very important during this year—she started me on music lessons with the old upright piano we had in the living room. It was a Star piano. The Star Company also manufactured refrigerators before going out of business. It was a sturdy piano, just right for a learner. This was very important to me because I learned the basics of music at an early age—the clefs, dominant chords, diminished minors, and the mathematics of everything musical. It was a whole new world unto itself, and I was being given the keys to something so vast and so beautiful.

My music teacher was Ms. Edith Robinson, who charged fifty cents for a lesson of half an hour. I had two lessons each week. That was somewhat of an accelerated pace, but it was just right for me at the time. I'm not sure I was what they call a gifted musician. But I did attract other students to Ms. Robinson. She was proud of me for doing this marketing job for her. One student in particular was Jack Mootz, who turned out to be a real dud on the piano. We never talked about him.

I would occasionally improvise, although she didn't like that very much. Music, to her, was written to be played. If it wasn't written, it wasn't to be played. I learned my music, as she instructed that year, and was thrilled by it all. Improvisation would come later, after I had stopped lessons. It was to be the bridge that kept my piano music alive—before I relearned what I had forgotten.

So the year following the breakup of my family was kept busy. I don't think of this period as a damaged situation. Things were as they were, and that was that.

Chapter 3
Grammar School
1939 to 1946

There were three consequences to the attempt to make me a model student: no sports, negotiate rather than fight, and my family would support a cultured education. They put me on a course that would prove to be difficult to manage. But I stayed on the course with support from my grandfather all the way.

The first was that there was no sports in this package. My grandfather took no interest in sports, and I took that as a signal that meant sports were unneeded. In fact, they appeared to be a cut below what it was that I was to be. In addition, I was not particularly gifted with physical strength or skill to be much of a sportsman. So sports passed by.

I did learn the rules of baseball, largely because the Cleveland Indians won the world series in 1948, and everybody in town talked baseball. You had to know baseball as the city went through this dizzy period. I still recall some of the arcane rules and exceptions to these rules, which added to the fun of the game. I never learned football and basketball rules so well, and I wish I did.

Being a nonplayer of games meant that I was somewhat of an outsider, which I didn't mind. It was as if I had a different call.

The second consequence was that I wouldn't fight. In the scrappy world of young boys aged six to nine years, there were always pokes and shoves and outright fights. These went on every day. One's status in the class and the neighborhood depended on those physical tryouts and were confirmed almost on a daily basis on the outcome. I was not part of this. Not being willing to fight meant I was in the sissy camp, and my punishment was to be jeered on frequent occasions. That didn't bother me much. I just walked by and paid no attention to it all.

My father was concerned. He felt something had to be done. At first he tried to get me to, as he would say, "Stand up for yourself." All of his advice went in one ear and out the other. I was taking a signal from my grandfather, who would simply look away. I knew he didn't approve, and that was good enough for me.

But my father was serious about the matter, and he took me to a gym, where people learned how to box with their fists and practiced their boxing in preparation of fights. This must have looked ludicrous—this nine-year-old kid in a boxing gym. In any event, I tried to do as I was instructed. I punched a duffle bag; I learned to posture to be on guard and how to punch with the right arm and the left arm, the various fakes, and the footwork. I learned it all, and one of the younger men pretended to box with me so I could be introduced into the real thing. This went on for several months, but my heart was not in any of the events. I couldn't get angry at my opponent and really disliked all of the shenanigans. Finally, my father gave up and considered the effort hopeless, and I was released from what had become a miserable experience. I still wouldn't fight.

The third consequence was that my family would support me in a cultured way of life. What this meant was that I would do as my grandfather would do. I should study art and draw to my heart's content.

The second grade through the sixth grade comprised the majority of my grammar school. I was not a stellar student. My grades were a touch above a gentleman's *C*. I didn't worry about this. I was getting by, and being average had its benefits. You didn't have to worry about letting people down with a lower grade. There were no real disappointments.

Grammar school began at Grant School, which carried me from first to fourth grades. This was the oldest school in Lakewood. It was two floors, with rooms on each floor arranged in a circle. At least once a week, all of the classes would gather in the center area and hear a song, a speech, or something of general interest. All four classes would congregate and to some extent intermingle. I liked the openness of this arrangement.

However, my final two years of grammar school were at Lincoln School, which had rooms in a row on two floors. There were no assemblies. Each class was tightly isolated. I felt I took a step backward in this school. Everyone was closely confined. I did not like Lincoln, but what could you do?

I didn't realize how important architecture and the layout of space were to living and learning until I left these two grammar schools. I didn't know any alternatives while I was there. I just did the best I could at the time. But I instinctively felt something had to be better.

I was one of the lucky kids who often had a bit of change in my pockets. On one occasion, this got me into a lot of trouble. It turned out that the patriotic effort during the Second World War carried down to the fifth grade at Lincoln, and everyone was supposed to buy at least one savings stamp for ten cents each week.

The savings stamps were pasted into a little booklet. The booklet had room for 187 stamps and was worth $18.70. When it was filled, you could take the booklet to a post office, add a nickel, and receive one war bond which could be redeemed in ten years for twenty-five dollars. It was one of the many ways the government financed the war.

There was a contest to see which room could reach the highest level of participation in buying these war stamps. Our room was in the middle, and my fifth grade teacher, Ms. Van Duser, talked to the class about finding an extra dime each Friday to boost the room's ranking. A big sheet of paper had been hung in the lobby of the school, and her name was on it also, with a middling rank. I suppose she wanted to be higher on the list. The answer was simple, I felt. I would lend anyone who needed a dime, and they could buy one of these war stamps and then pay me back the following week.

All went well for a couple of weeks. Suddenly our classroom had 100 percent participation. We shot to the top of the list. Nice words were spoken about our class, and Ms. Van Duser was walking around with her head up in the air. Then it became clear to me that something was wrong. A number of classmates who had borrowed a dime each week were not paying me back, as they were supposed to. And they didn't seem worried about this. My problem was that I wanted my money back, but I didn't want to get anybody upset.

It turned out that all of this happened near Valentine's day, February 14, and at this time, everybody made valentines which were sent in a pretend post box to everybody else. I decided to include a past-due bill in each of the nonpayers. It would be a written reminder in a quiet sort of way. Or so I thought. Most everybody took these valentines home to show their parents what they had done. So far, so good. But I still didn't have my dimes back.

Then when some of the parents saw my due-bills, they hit the ceiling. Three mothers stormed into Ms. Van Duser's class. Others went to see our principal, Mr. Clark. How could they allow such a thing? They were condoning low-down loan activities. Negative comments were coming toward me a mile a minute. Then Ms. Van Duser gave me one of her steel-blue eye contacts which said it was all over. I was the cause of her enormous embarrassment. Her class ranking went from the top to near the bottom on the school banner.

There was no place to hide. I even thought of trying to climb inside my small desk. But deep down, I wondered what was so wrong about this. It was a risky venture. I could lose my money. And the penny a week interest that I charged was a small amount, I felt. At the time, nobody thought about what that would mean in rate of interest terms. Somehow, somebody paid me back, but with no interest, and I was in the doghouse for the rest of the semester.

When I would visit my mother's sister, my aunt Jean, I liked to give my cousin Judy wagon rides. Away we would go down the street. I pretended we were on a street car, and we went across the street to another block. There was a little mom and pop store that sold ice cream cones. You got two scoops for a nickel.

Then one day, the owner said you get only one scoop for a nickel. I was outraged and had a little scene. But there was nothing I could do, except forget about ice cream, and I didn't want that. This was my first encounter with inflation. I have never liked inflation ever after.

When I visited my aunt Jean, I would play with John and Judy. John had his friends, and I would join them. Because I was John's cousin, I was accepted. I even batted a ball through a window—crash—and we all ran for home, hoping to get out of sight before we were discovered. We didn't escape. News of it all was waiting for us when we arrived at the house.

My grandmother was my friend and protector. She stood tall as she upheld her basic beliefs of honesty and fairness. I learned from her what it meant to be a gentleman. Only once did we cross our paths. And that was over religion.

She wanted me to join the Lakewood Methodist Church, which happened at the time to be the largest in the land. I had no interest in joining and thought that most of the members were hypocrites. I saw many church members drinking, playing cards, smoking, and heaven knows what else. All of these were prohibited. But more to the heart of the matter, I couldn't see how any of this had anything to do with religion or more, to the essence of it all, to spirituality, which I regarded as being the core of religion.

But I agreed to go to a prep school that taught us what we were supposed to know. That only postponed the trouble. Anything, anything to postpone what was bound to be a showdown. And all of this over religion, of all things.

The moment of truth came when our religion class stood up in church and marched to the front to receive the minister, Reverend Fallon—everyone but me. I sat in the pew, glued to the spot. I also had a personal reason to keep my seat. The Rev. Fallon spoke ill of his divorced wife. I didn't like that.

For three months afterward, my grandmother was like ice. That hurt. But after a long while, the matter faded. I have never been happy with this occasion. It might not have been worth it all.

My grandparents liked to take me to visit relatives in Twinsburg, where my deceased Uncle Avery's family lived. His daughter, Pat, had four children near my age: Averill, Craig,

Laurie, and George. Pat always had a smile, like her mother, Aunt Hulda. Aunt Hulda had kept her family together by starting a lunchroom at the bank Uncle Avery had worked, the Central National Bank.

The family loves to tell the story about me when I went to the store to buy candy and never ate a meal for a couple of days. Then at dinner and without warning, I threw up all over the table and was completely humiliated. But the family only remembered the funny part of this story. It shows their inherent good nature.

Another member of this family, my uncle Dave, was a wonderful friend. He gave me a ride in the family's 1940 Ford, which was quite a thrill, since he was the local high school basketball star, and the car was the hottest model on the road. All the ladies would kid him about who his girlfriend might be; Dave never liked this, but it was the price you paid for being tall, trim, and a sportsman. In later years, Dave felt my grandfather had not helped him all that he might. I don't know much about that. But I think that Dave, like most people, thought he was wealthy, when he actually was in debt; I admired Dave and always liked visiting these wonderful relatives.

Sometimes I needed special tutoring. This was always couched in upbeat terms. It wasn't that I was dumb, stupid, but a little boost would make everybody happy. So I went to Ms. Robinson's sister to learn English a bit better. I thoroughly enjoyed the tutoring and was very disappointed when I was told I had done well enough and need not continue. On another occasion, I had not learned my multiplication tables very thoroughly. My father took up this tutoring assignment, and every time we got into his car, he started drilling me on these numbers. It was a bit like a sport, and I loved those challenges and also was sad when they stopped.

But on the whole, grammar school was quite dreary. Classes were sullen, and my teachers, almost every one of them, were autocratic. Order was required, and any variation from the order set down by the teacher brought terrible humiliation. And there was always the punishment of being sent to the office of the principal. That meant a call from the principal and bad news when you got home.

The overall mission of the school was to impart basic knowledge into the minds of a bunch of vacant heads, and mine was one of them. I was not happy. I was not unhappy. I got along. There was nothing in school—sports or lessons—that grabbed my interest.

My fifth grade teacher, Ms. Van Duser, was typical of what I faced every day. I always remember that name because it seemed to be out of a novel.

Ms. Van Duser caught me riding my bicycle to school one day. This was a major infraction of the rules. I can't remember why it was so bad, but anyway, I was in deep trouble. Ms. Van Duser made a spectacle of me in front of the class and then sent me to the principal. I sat in his outer office, trembling at what my fate would be. He called my grandfather—he must not have been able to reach my father—and I heard this self-righteous bureaucrat's voice change from one being in charge to one who took orders.

It turned out that my grandfather said there was nothing written or implied that would prohibit my riding a bicycle to school and that he would see to it that I should be able to do so. Of course, my admiration for my grandfather zoomed. And my faith in officialdom went lower. When I returned to Ms. Van Duser's class, it was as if nothing had happened. There was no explanation, no apology, just a brusque business-as-usual demeanor.

I had pushed the envelope a bit far. I had recently received my bicycle for Christmas, and I was very proud of it. The make was a Raleigh, an English bike which was a showpiece. The bicycle was also a bagful of trouble and needing constant repairs. Still, these were moments of triumph, which made up for the humdrum, ordinary days.

There were exceptions. Ms. Hoskins taught writing, or penmanship, as it was sometimes called. Ms. Hoskins was a "with it" young lady of about thirty years and a bright cheerful smile. I liked her, as did her class. She made learning seem easy.

She told everyone what was special about them, kept emphasizing strengths, and celebrated each person's success. What a teacher. My grades improved in her class, as did most other members of her class. It wasn't grade inflation; it was genuine improvement.

Ms. Hoskins went on to become a principal somewhere, and what a lucky school that was.

It also happened that my father dated this wonderful teacher. As I recall, he dated her for half of a year. I don't recall what happened, but I was sorry to see her go. The last date he had with her, he had bought a used 1936 Chevrolet coupe, and he was as delighted as a true car buff. He was particularly proud of the hydraulic brakes, which he said would "really" stop the car. He also kept telling me how much easier it was to repair compared with his Ford. In those days everybody liked to talk about cars, and every man and boy knew their cars down to the spark plugs. This was especially true, I read somewhere, in Detroit, Cleveland, and Akron, where most cars were made.

Outside of school, I was building model airplanes, which I adored. I kept building bigger and bigger model planes. At one point, there was not enough room in my bedroom to place them all. How proud I was of those planes. I wonder where they all went.

From time to time, I would take my wagon to the grocery store a block away and ask for any wood orange crates. In those days, oranges were shipped in wooden containers, not the cardboard ones used today. I would take the claw side of a hammer, remove the nails, and take the wagon, which was now full of wood, to a street corner and offer the wood for fifteen cents a packet. That included seven thin boards and two inch-thick small boards.

Some passersby were bemused and bought some of my wood out of amusement. Others used it as kindling. We still had half the houses heated with fire-burning coal at that time.

Still, others used it in their fireplaces. One man trounced my efforts by telling me that I was only selling crate wood which was worthless. He said even the grocery stores didn't want that junk, as he put it. I was crushed after hearing that and went home right away. He was right. But he was also wrong. I had prepared the wood in a packet which was convenient for him to handle and store. I didn't think of that at the time. Anyway, my little business didn't go anywhere.

In addition, I organized a small group of friends into what I named the Korny Club. We sat around a table and cut out cartoons from newspapers, magazines, and whatever we could find and pasted them into a booklet. We often had heated discussions about cartoons that were candidates for being included in this very exclusive book.

Since there were seldom more than four or five of us at a sitting, there was always plenty of time—and room—for discussion. But for the most part, the sessions were amicable. I always had an enjoyable time. Little did I know that this plaything of my childhood would be the essence of my later business report called the *Money Analyst*.

In the second grade, I started piano lessons. As I mentioned earlier, my teacher was the spinster sister of my first grade teacher. My grandmother knew her through the Eastern Star, which was the women's equivalent to the Masons of the men.

Our piano at home was an upright, a little rattly, and had a few chips, like most old furniture. It could never hold a tune and sounded terrible. My grandmother took some of the money she inherited from the sale of Uncle Ruff's farm and bought me a new Wurlizer piano, a baby grand, which was very generous. But sad to say, this new piano didn't sound much better. But I was polite and thanked her many times.

Ms. Robinson was patient and immensely knowledgeable. She not only showed me what the notes on a staff sounded like, but the whole business of expression, the meaning of the Italian words that are so prevalent in classical music. She gave me all of the greats to learn. It was like opening a treasure chest, and there I was standing before all of this, a little kid.

I practiced regularly and could play a number of pieces from memory without making too many mistakes. But by junior high school, my interest waned, and by the time high school was on the scene, I stopped taking lessons. Ms. Robinson was disappointed, but she knew what was competing for my time at school was irresistible. Piano playing was lonely time, and the school activities—except choir—didn't have any place for it.

But before Ms. Robinson said I would be released from her instruction, as she put it, I would have to learn Schumann's short piece called *Traumerei*. This turned out to be prophetic, as this was the piece I turned to many years later when I took up piano playing once again. This piece is a gem. I now feel it is the finest romantic work ever written.

In the fifth and sixth grades, one of the girls in the class, Betty De Beck, caught my eye. Betty was a vivacious girl, and whenever she was around, you could be sure of a good time. She had a way about her that people always wanted to join in and do the things she wanted to do. I was not alone in liking her, but I always felt I was a little extra special in her book. Maybe this was self-delusion, but it was nice.

In the back of our house was a large field which somehow had escaped being developed. It was really a beautiful forest with a large lake near the middle. The shore of this lake was full of small creatures, including frogs, flying insects, and strange-sounding somethings that made croaking sounds. It was a magic place.

It was also a place of dreams. You could take a walk to this woods and to the lake, and all of the mean things of the world would disappear.

I would draw a map of this woods and assign portions to various friends. All of this was imaginary, and I never mentioned it to the people who were assigned mythical territories. I knew it was farfetched, and the fun would be spoiled if people knew I was doing such a ditzy thing. Then I would pretend there was a war between these territories. The war was fought with imaginary snowballs and row boats. Only kids played in this war, and nobody got hurt. Tactics were endless, and with even more imagination, it could be played anywhere.

Turkey Foot Lake was my idea of heaven. On very special Saturdays, my father would take me there. This was really a collection of lakes with interconnecting canals. We would rent a rowboat and spend the day or until five o'clock, when the boats had to be returned. We would take turns, and my father always tried to show off a bit by pulling harder than I could. This never bothered me. I was happy for him and thought that someday I too could be that strong.

Turkey Foot Lake was a life savior at times. My grandfather's idea of recreation was a Sunday drive—really to nowhere. I would sit in the backseat, next to my father. My grandmother sat on the passenger side of the front seat, and of course, my grandfather took the helm on the left side. I would usually get slightly car sick from the soft suspension of the car, which was a Packard. If we came near this lake, I would put up a protest on the ride and ask to let my father and me out to row a boat. This was fine for everybody, and it was wonderful relief for me.

When my father got out on the water, a wonderful transformation came over him. He was inwardly happy, I felt, and he could then be quite patient, quite different than he was when he fixed his car. One time, on the lake, I began to rock the boat, just for fun. My father, in a very patient voice—I can hear him now—cautioned me not to do this, since the boat would capsize. I didn't listen, and the boat did capsize. All of the contents, including my father's imported German camera went to the bottom of the lake. He was very gentle and simply told me that was what happens when you do things like that. I was struck dumb. He was so gentle about this loss. I didn't know what to say. I still don't know what to say, and that time has long gone away.

Another favorite place to visit was Cook's Forest, just over the state line into Pennsylvania. This was in rolling hills, full of big maple trees and oaks, and near Oil City, where the oil industry began. My father would save up gasoline coupons, so we would be able to make the one-hundred mile trip each way. These were rationing coupons, and a *C* packet was the most generous. He would ride his motorcycle to save his gasoline for trips like that.

I was most appreciative and also most proud of my father in the second grade. I was given the lead part in a Christmas play titled something like *No Room at the Inn*. I played the part of the innkeeper. My father took time off his work and dressed up in his best blue suit. He looked just right, and he spoke nicely to the teachers who were present.

My father also took me on long trips. We put boards over the car seats and had a tight cabin, but it was just fine as a place to sleep. We traveled this way to Oklahoma to visit one of my grandfather's clients who was the head of an oil company. From Oklahoma, we went to Dallas. I remember how friendly strangers were and how much I admired the common courtesies of letting other people go through a door first. My dad never wanted to stop for anything. I frequently kept asking him to stop at a restroom, but to little avail until I made a ruckus. He never liked to stop for food, either. So traveling with him had certain drawbacks. But he was a good companion on trips, always ready to explore something interesting. He had a curious mind.

I have always been amazed at the number of senior executives that my grandfather knew. He planned their trusts and became a senior and trusted advisor ever after. Everyone spoke well of him. This trip was just before the Second World War.

Another trip was to New York City during the war. We went on to Washington DC, but I came down with a bad cold and stayed in the hotel room while my father went on a drive with Bill Dixon, a lawyer who was one of my grandfather's best friends. Again and again, my grandfather's reach kept impressing me. He said he would introduce me to his friends when I grew up, but that never happened. By that time, they had all retired or had died. It was an illusion that these men would help me, but at the time, I believed it.

The Second World War had little impact on my life—but it came very close. There was rationing of meat, butter, and gasoline, but this was not serious. And restaurants had all the meat and butter you would want.

Yet there was a close scrape. My father was called up for a physical examination, and his chart had already designated him to be sent to the navy, so it was a serious moment. It was 1942, and manpower was desperately needed to fight the war, especially in the Pacific, as the navy was fighting for survival. Even though my grandfather was chairman of the local draft board number 30, he couldn't intervene. The die was cast.

But he had feet that were too flat. He was rejected for service as being unfit and given a 4F classification for the remainder of the war.

Chapter 4
Junior High School
1946 to 1949

Junior High School was freedom to me. The oppression of dictator teachers was gone. We went to five or six teachers each day in different rooms. There was no big boss. The homeroom teacher was supposed to be the coordinator but never went beyond that weak supervisory role.

This meant I could go for the most in each class. It meant that I could push, make a fool out of myself, and say my mind without fear of being shot down and then having to sit at the same place, quietly, while a dictatorship asserted its limitations.

All of that old stuff was gone. Whoever I might be—I could be just that. Nothing could have been more wonderful.

First of all, I was happy. Second, for some unexplained reason, my grades improved. I was still a slow poke in Latin, but everything else was pretty close to *A* level. What good news this was. I had never thought of myself as a scholar, and now something like that had happened.

Then something strange happened, which I have never understood. The principal at Horace Mann Junior High School was Cecil Casper Clark, who always signed his name with the initials, CCC. He asked my father to come to the school and, according to what my father said, reviewed my work and said that I was of ordinary intelligence, but I worked very hard, was motivated, and due to that effort, my grades were high.

My father took this as a source of pride. I got the feeling that Mr. Clark meant it to mean that my natural endowment was nothing to write home about and that nobody should get excited about any grades that might be good. That was the way officials think, or so I thought.

But my reaction to this news was that this was terrific. It meant that I would not be bound by so-called natural endowment, but that I could reach for the stars and grab them through my own efforts. It fitted into the scheme of things that my grandfather had in mind when he set me up to be a model student.

At the time, I hadn't all of this worked out, rather it all seemed to be the way things were meant to be. And it was the way I would move ahead. No amount of hardship or difficulty would stand in the way. Effort and perseverance could push the obstacles—whatever they might be—aside. It was a heady point of view. From that point on, my future would lie in my hands. If I were to fail, I would have nobody but myself to blame.

I would later learn, at great pain, that this was not always true.

At that point, the key would be school grades. They were the single, most universal indicator. My efforts would be to score high.

The idea of college came into mind at this time. It was still a vague idea, but the idea that there were a few best colleges became something to think about. Our next-door neighbors, Mr. and Mrs. Norman Bill, began to talk to me about Princeton University. They had lived there when they were young and, on that basis, recommended it.

This meant that things that I had been doing that were not related to grades would have to be stopped, and the time would be used to support superior grades. So out went efforts at painting. Out went piano lessons. Actually, I had progressed nicely in piano playing. I had learned Beethoven's *Moonlight Sonata* and Schumann's *Traumeri*, as well as other pieces. I was never good at sight reading, but I could memorize scores with some ease. My grandmother was disappointed when I stopped taking lessons. She had bought me a Wurlizer baby grand a few years before and harbored hopes, I suspect, that I had some major talent in music. The money for the piano, I believed, had come from a small inheritance from her uncle, when his farm near Oberlin had been sold.

That uncle was Uncle Ruff, short for Rufus. He and his wife opened their farm to all of the city folks, as we were called, every fourth of July. It was a picnic, and all of the ladies brought their best dishes. My grandmother always brought a Jell-O salad with cottage cheese, which everybody exclaimed was delicious. I remember that my grandfather always arrived with a white shirt, tie, and suit and took off his coat when the day heated up but never took off his tie. There was lots of talk about politics and weather and crops. I liked these days. They were lazy, dreamy days with friendly people.

Uncle Ruff sold an acre of his farm to my aunt Ethel, who was my grandmother's sister. Aunt Ethel was a story in itself. She had married Uncle Paul, who emigrated from Germany during the great inflation and depression in that country following the First World War. He was a builder by trade, and Aunt Ethel was a society lady. What a combination. Both were complete characters.

Aunt Ethel was a member of two very conservative patriotic societies for ladies. The first was the Daughters of the American Revolution, which is often designated as the DAR. She attended local and regional meetings of this society. But her real claim to fame was that she was state regent of the Daughters of the American Colonists or the DAC. Your ancestors had to have been here before the American Revolution to belong to that one. And to be the ranking state official meant something in upper social circles.

So Aunt Ethel would load up her car once a year with three of her pals and drive to Washington DC to attend meetings. They would arrive back home full of spunk on how to revive the country's original spirit, whatever that meant. But it was a wonderful thing to see my aunt Ethel go beyond her small house out in the farmland of Ohio to take on national concerns.

I laughed a little bit when all of this was mentioned, but I was truly proud of her and proud to be connected with her.

Uncle Paul was famous in our family for his cement bathtubs. He also wrote books about how people evolved from animals and the top people came from lions. Mere peasants descended from something else. One book, *On Trails of Fire*, was passed around with a wink. I tried to read it but couldn't understand it. It was all good fun to talk about, and Uncle Paul was always pleasant to me. We did have to keep him indoors during the Second World War, when the Allied armies were sweeping across France, and he said they would never cross the Rhine. Nobody got worried about this. We knew things would turn out okay, and when the war was over, all would be forgotten. It was.

Every family needs some people who are a bit nutty, and they certainly qualified. It was a shame they never had any children. Children from parents like those two often turn out to be remarkable people who do very individual things.

In the eighth grade, my grandfather received a gift of a chow dog from a business associate. I suspect that this friend was raising the dogs. This was not unusual, since my grandfather had business arrangements outside the bank during this period. In particular, he secured automobile dealerships for interested parties. My father and I even made a trip to Miami, Florida, to look over prospects for one dealership.

That led to an excursion to Cuba, which was my first experience in a foreign country. Cuba was exotic. It was full of fantastically beautiful music with soaring flutes and rhythms that made you want to dance. It was also the location of the Hotel Nacional, which had the most wonderful coconut ice cream in a coconut shell. Yet I felt it was all temporary. I knew I would return to reality at home soon enough.

My grandfather wanted me to be an artist. He harbored some secret yearnings to lead this life and create something heroic and personal. That was who he was. So he bought me lots of oil paints and all kinds of brushes and set me to it. Well, I painted, but even I thought it was simply awful. That Christmas I gave everybody an oil painting. The only person who called it as it was was Mother, who said the picture couldn't go on her walls.

I also enrolled in art classes for young people. It was fun, but I could see others had more talent than I did. One member of this class, Laurence was his first name and I forgot his last name, had real talent. I admired him immensely. No, I envied him. Why couldn't I have this talent? Then grandfather would have been proud, and I would have found my field. Instead, I would sit in front of my canvas or paper and ask myself—how did Laurence know where to put this line or where did the idea for a particular color come from? I was over my head.

Grandfather didn't give up easily. He even had some fine artists as well as some commercial artists over to our house. He took my work to their studios. It was to no avail. I wasn't a future artist. I will never forget Mr. Rappaport of Rappaport Studios harrumph and almost laugh at my painting, as he pronounced it very low art. It was hard to take, disappointing grandfather.

But this was just the beginning. I was not the person nor the talent he wanted me to be.

My grandfather also talked about moving to a larger home on Lake Avenue, which was a prestigious address. But the money came in and went out. He made what amounted to small change for his efforts outside the bank. His visions were bright, but the reality was small. Yet he was always full of optimism. His motto, which I admire and often repeat, is that the best is yet to come.

Anyway, back to the chow dog, whom I named Chang. I liked Chang, especially when he was a puppy. He was manageable. We made a pen for him to live between our garage and our neighbor's garage, the one owned by Mr. and Mrs. Bill. As he got bigger, I had a hard time taking him for walks and didn't tend to him as much as he would like. Then he got large enough to jump over his fence, and nobody made the fence higher. So he began to escape, and I would search the neighborhood for him. One day, he was sick, and we took him to the veterinary doctor and left him. I would stop to see him on the way home from school, but he didn't seem to be getting better.

A few days later, Ms. Marie Disney, the assistant principal at Horace Mann Junior High School sought me out of a class and said that my grandmother had asked me to come straight home, which I did. Then I was told that Chang had died. I was grief stricken and burst into tears that would not go away. Chang was getting to be too big, and he was a task and a half. But I loved him. He was my dog, and dogs are best friends when you need them. They are always there for you, devoted. I felt terrible feelings of guilt that I had let Chang down. And I had. And there was nothing I could do at this point. I kept saying, "Why, oh why, oh why, oh why?" There was no answer. To this day, there is no answer.

Later, Mrs. Bill told me that she heard that a neighbor down the street disliked Chang because he left markings in her yard. She added that she believed that the neighbor poisoned Chang. This was terrible to hear. I took this news quietly like a big weight. It was all over. Nothing could be done. It was my first experience with grief.

One day, when I was in the ninth grade, my father complained of being dizzy. I was fifteen years old. He then threw up and went to bed and stayed there for several days. We all became concerned. My grandmother was particularly worried. My grandfather called in a doctor against my father's wishes. The doctor said my father had Meniere's disease, and that it would pass. There was no improvement for several more days, and so my grandfather put my father in his car and drove him to the Cleveland Clinic. There, the diagnosis was much more serious. They took X-rays and said he had an aneurysm in his head artery. Aneurysms are 90 percent fatal. I didn't know this at the time, but the deep concern was enough to tell me that he was deathly ill.

The doctors kept him in the hospital for about a week, watching him. They did not want to operate to try to repair this tear in the artery because of the risk of uncontrollable bleeding. I would go to see him each day, driving his car. I was fifteen years old. In those days, the law was more relaxed about driving licenses, or so our family believed. That couldn't happen today. And I was a careful driver.

My father recovered gradually. He had been a welder during the war. My grandfather filled his head with dreams of becoming a banker. And my grandfather even got him a job in the Lorain Street Bank near our home. He was a payroll teller right off the bat. This is the teller's teller, and it was a job for which he lacked experience. So it didn't last very long. Then he became a stockbroker with a high-tension brokerage firm, Prescott & Co. It was the firm that floated Kaiser-Frasier stock, which was a company that manufactured cars for a few years after the war, before it went broke. Then Prescott & Co. went broke. Needless to say, that didn't work out.

So my father took a hint from one of his old buddies, Ed Robinson, and decided to drive a semitruck. These are the engine and front of the large cargo trucks we see on the highway. My grandfather was very disappointed, but my father felt liberated. He was pretty much his own boss; the pay was good, and he was near engines, which he really liked. Our neighbors didn't know what to think. They thought of their domain as one of quiet refinement, even if there wasn't much money. First, motorcycles, then trucks. Where would it end? He liked that kind of gossip, which he could thumb his nose at. But he never did this openly.

Still, the job of being a truck driver carried an image of something low class. I never was comfortable saying he was a truck driver, simply because he was a much more advanced person than what the popular image conveyed. So I settled on calling him a contract hauler, which is quite correct. Most people didn't know what this was but seldom asked me to explain it. When they did, I simply said it involved trucks, and they left it at that.

My pals often tried out junkets. One was to visit the steel mills in the flats of Cleveland, near the Cuyahoga River. Claude Rust, Bill Deibel, Jack Swanson and I would climb in my dad's 1946 Ford, and we would gape in wonder at the power of a steel mill, with all of its fire and heat. In those days, you could do this sort of thing.

My grandfather and grandmother kept hatching ideas for me to play out. One of the most outlandish was for me to study magic. I was to become an amateur magician, because magicians were always in demand, regardless of the group, and they could use this talent to be popular. My study of magic was very elementary, but it was arranged that a magician named Mr. Seymour would stop at the house to see me perform. It was a shambles, but everyone pretended the show was great. I had prepared ice water for refreshments, and Mr. Seymour thought the drinks were a hoot. He intimated that he would have preferred something much stronger. It was my introduction to the world of drinks. Anyway, my magic days were over.

My grandfather was at his prime in this period, just after the Second World War. He took me along on many of his business trips. Sometimes he introduced me to his customers, but usually, he left me to explore the city on my own. These were interesting cities like Detroit and Chicago. The cities of the Midwest were at their peak at this time, and their wealth spilled over into the arts and sciences. I remember being dazzled at the Science and Industry museum in Chicago, which showed a model steam engine and the way it worked. The museum also had a reconstructed coal mine.

We stayed at the best place in town—the Union League Club, where I saw a businessman cash a check for one hundred dollars. I thought to myself why in the world anybody would need that much money. When we went to Detroit, we went on the *D&C Line*, which was a steamboat that took passengers overnight from Cleveland to Detroit. My grandfather was a bit put out that I wanted the lower berth. He apparently, I later gathered, did not enjoy climbing down from above. At the time, I never thought about these things.

Boys were getting together with girls. In my class, we had Jay Sweet and Marilyn Kelsey who set the pace. They were what we called fast ones. Jay was the best baseball player in the class. It was truly amazing to see him peg a baseball precisely to a teammate seventy feet away. He nearly always could bat himself to first base. Marilyn was fully developed so far as the boys were concerned. There was a lot of speculation about what might be going on between the two of them. And as the ninth grade progressed, the girls held parties for the boys. I went to a few of these parties but was never caught up in the swing of things.

I did try to have a party of my own, which ended in the dumps. During the week before the party, I had a rough time and wasn't very nice to my family. Grandmother had enough of my acting up and told me the party wouldn't occur. This meant that I would have to cancel it. I felt let down and embarrassed but did my duty and told everyone the party was off. I was concerned, but nobody else was concerned. At the hour that the party was to begin, I was in a deep depression. After that, I have never liked to cancel a party.

My piano playing did serve me well in an incident that many friends, including Claude Rust, remind me of. The school had an amateur contest, and I entered as a piano player. I was the third of four people who performed on the piano. The first two sat down on the piano bench, and it squeaked loudly, with the sound echoing throughout the auditorium. I arrived on the scene with a big oilcan and turned the piano bench on its side and oiled it. The squeak went away, and there was thunderous laughter and applause. It was my finest hour.

All of this activity meant that I became well-known. I spoke up outside the classroom and inside the classroom. I discovered that grades were heavily weighted by classroom participation. There was no such thing as bad contributions. There were only contributions or no contributions, and I was at the forefront of making contributions. I also learned that in the end, the point of view mattered little. The teacher's point of view would prevail. Power has its prerogatives.

Chapter 5
Senior High School
1949 to 1952

The path of junior high school ran through high school. It was a time where the sky was the limit.

The major difference was the much greater extent of things to do. First, there were sports. There were teams for everything, or so it seemed. And the teams were eager to recruit teammates, no matter how clumsy you might be. The junior teams for the tenth graders were called J-V teams, which was short for junior varsity teams. I joined the track team. My runs were the one-hundred and two-hundred-yard dashes. Coach Antel also wanted me to run the quarter-mile sprint.

The dashes were a piece of cake, but the quarter miler—well, that was quite a race. I would finish panting like a hound dog. My interest in track waned as the days grew colder. Then at our meet in mid-October, it began to snow. We were freezing in our wraps, then we stripped to our running outfits and braved the snowflakes. This was not fun.

So I told Coach Antel I needed extra time for my studies, and I wouldn't be on the team any longer. He had heard this story many times before, I'm sure, and told me the team needed me. I wasn't firm enough and was still on the team, that is, until the next meet where there wasn't snow but a twenty-mile-an-hour headwind, which froze just about everyone. That did it for me. I was off the team because I simply didn't show up. I always liked Coach Antel and was sorry that we parted this way.

But I got no support at home for athletics. In fact, it was as if I had gone off course in my grandmother's thinking. Perhaps I should have tried a team sport, indoors, like basketball. It would have been worth a try.

But there was a more important reason that I didn't follow sports. The clubs that met at the same time as sports held practice were more interesting to me. And I wasn't able to do both because there wasn't enough time for both.

Moreover, you were a sports person or a club person in extracurricular activities. People in one circle didn't mix with the other circle. If you were in one of these, you could travel in other teams or be an accepted guest in another club. You were accepted.

But as was mentioned, the clubs and sports didn't mix. That was too bad.

By the end of my first semester in high school, I had joined three clubs and enjoyed every minute.

The most important was Hi-Forum, which was the social studies club. The club was overseen by Margaret Warner, who was the most affirmative and outspoken social studies teacher. She was also a strong socialist, and that had to be reckoned with because my instincts were much more conservative. I handled this by keeping my political views to myself but made up for this omission in her eyes by working hard for the club. That was enough to cement a great relationship that lasted until she died some years later. And it was an important relationship. Margaret Warner was my advocate in the school, and she always spoke up for me. I am very grateful to her.

She also had favors to dispense. The two prizes were Buckeye Boys State and the trip to visit the United Nations in New York City. She chose me for both.

The Buckeye Boys State was a week at a former army camp where juniors in high school created a mock state government. Everybody arrived as a citizen and then started campaigning to get elected to some office. Right away, it was clear that groups from mid and south counties of Ohio had made deals for the high offices.

I decided to run for supreme court justice, figuring that I had the best chance of winning one of the seven seats, and it would be a fun job. So I met everyone I could find and asked them for their support, and "Please," I would say, "remember my name." I passed out little cards, which most people threw away. But that was all right. Enough people kept the cards or remembered my name for me to get elected. The night of my inauguration, my father drove up with my grandparents in a surprise visit. They told me how proud they were. And it was a good moment for me.

The trip to the United Nations involved seeing the General Assembly in its deliberations and seeing where the Security Council met. It was all done in almost hushed reverence. It also had the effect of reaffirming the importance of the United Nations as a major force in American foreign policy—always for the good of mankind. Nobody on the trip questioned this doctrine.

One memorable time on the trip was a dinner in an Indian restaurant. My tastes in food had not broadened at all, and I didn't enjoy the dinner. But it opened my eyes to the fact that cultures were often different in a dramatic way and showed me this better than any speech or learned article.

Kaythryn Moore was the teacher for public speaking. She was the school's leading character. She always spoke to you as if she were addressing a throng of people. She was a short lady with powerful convictions and bright red or blue or some other colored hair, depending on the day. She would conduct the speaking class as a baptism of fire. She told the timid boys and girls to stand on the stage alone and then told them to start speaking. More than one girl broke down in tears, but it worked. By the end of the semester, even the most retiring person could get on the stage and say at least their name.

This course was great fun for me. The prize was to win a contest to represent the school in the Lake Erie League speech contest. I tried out for this and came in second. That meant that I was the alternate and got to make the trip without having to do anything. The winner to represent our school was Jack Swanson, who was a close friend and a truly distinguished orator. On the appointed day for the league contest, Ms. Moore, Jack, and I traveled to Shaw High School in East Cleveland for the contest. There, to my surprise and delight, representing Shaw was my first cousin John Weedon. I remember John's speech teacher really liked John and wanted to help him in every way possible, and I thought this was the way a coach should be. At that moment, I thought Kaythryn Moore's approach of dumping people into the water and letting them swim was all wet. Jack didn't win, and John didn't win. I forgot who did.

There was something special about being the winner of the school's public speaking. I recalled earlier winners, including John Martindale (who went to Harvard and then left in his sophomore year) and Bruce Cook (who was two years ahead of me, went to Columbia and then joined the CIA). They all had great presence. They could say something simple, like it is raining today, and somehow, it sounded eventful and important. And they always were well organized. They were quiet leaders of school. They never ran for school office, but they were people you turned to when you had a problem. All of this made me realize that public speaking was somehow very important.

I did run for school office. I never won. It was a great experience. You were required to reach out and ask somebody you didn't know for support. That takes effort and a frame of mind that isn't easy to do without motivation. I found the first person of the day that I asked was the hardest. Just getting started was the whole battle. Then it was easy. You just kept on going.

In a way, the school elections were a type of freedom for me. I could reach out, with nobody saying no to me. I had a platform; I had something to say, and there I was, free as a bird. This principle held true everywhere at all times. It was wonderful. This is what freedom is all about.

My circle of friends broadened in the first year of high school. One friend, Bruce Bauman, helped introduce me to club members. He seemed to know everyone. In addition, his father was a fairly high manager at a General Motors plant, and every year, he got a new car. When I met Bruce, he was driving his dad's 1949 Buick Roadmaster—the car with four portholes, dynaflow transmission, and so long as not to fit on our driveway. In those days, cars were everything, and this car was a beauty. It was light, gunmetal grey. It was sheer pleasure to ride in it. And of course, it was the height of elegance to be seen riding in it.

The next year, Bruce's dad brought home a Cadillac coupe with so many bells and whistles I couldn't keep up with all of them. It was over the top. One feature was a radio that sought out stations. This was in a car when many cars had no radio at all. Mother's car didn't have a radio. Nobody today knows what excitement cars brought to our lives. Or how we all went to the dealer's showroom to admire the new models when they were just announced. My father and I spent many Saturday afternoons walking around new cars in showrooms, sharing our admiration of this and that. It was lots of fun to be with him on these journeys.

Every day, it seemed as if there was some high jinx that was played out. One of the most elaborate of these involved five of our group and the girls' swimming club called the Tankateers. This group involved beautiful patterns in the water through perfect formations by the girls. Five of the fellows, including Tom Brandt and Jim Barker, cooked up the idea that one of us would jump in the middle of a flower just as the Tankateers reached the climax of their show to the school. To make it worthwhile, each of us put up five dollars and took a straw. The loser, or winner, would get the money and suffer the brunt of whatever might happen. Jim Barker pulled the shortest straw and became the man to do the task. At the appointed moment, as the recorded music reached a crescendo and the girls formed a perfect flower, Jim climbed up the diving board and jumped into the center of the pool making a gigantic cannonball spectacle. Everyone laughed and hooted—everyone except the school officials, who didn't like this at all.

Jim was hauled off to the assistant principal's office to await his fate. This task was cut out for Mr. Robert L. Meeks, who in many ways fitted his name. He later told me he was so mad at Jim that he kept him waiting in a chair outside his office so he would not say anything that he shouldn't. He said that Jim then so charmed him that he later wrote a recommendation for Jim which helped him win a scholarship to Columbia. In whatever he did, Jim came out a winner.

During most of the time in high school, I dated Kay Huxtable. This wasn't a big romance, more like teenagers going together as part of a group. But Kay liked me a lot, and I liked her too. I think she liked me more than I liked her. She wanted me to take her out more often than school parties. And I think the family liked me.

There were all kinds of hints from her father, who was a very wealthy real estate tycoon in the Lakewood area. He always surprised me with something that was supposed to catch my eye. One time, I arrived at her house to take her to a prom, I said hello to everyone, and as we left to go to my rumbly Ford, Mr. Huxtable walked out to the driveway where a large limo was parked, and he said, "Here, use Mr. Codrington's car this evening. He's staying home this evening and wanted you to have it." We sure did arrive in style and went to the after-hours parties like royalty. The hint was not missed. Mr. Codrington was a General Motors vice president, and that was a time when titles were scarce, and GM meant something.

Another time, he took me into his den, opened up a box that held sheet after sheet of IBM stock, and said something about thrift. I simply kept calm, which made him think more so that I was the right man for his daughter.

Kay was a gem, a very lovely and gracious girl. She was everything right. But I felt I was too young to get attached, so after high school, we went our separate ways. She went to Cornell and studied medicine.

In my junior year, my grandmother became sick. She had difficulty swallowing, and after some time, she went to a doctor who sent her to the Cleveland Clinic. She waited several months before going to a doctor. This was not unusual. Most people didn't want to spend the money for a doctor's visit, and our family was no exception. And most people were afraid of doctors. They were worried what the doctor might find.

The Cleveland Clinic did find something bad. Grandmother had cancer of the throat. I wasn't told this at the time. That was in keeping with the great tradition of keeping any illness a secret; as if illness were some sort of wrong you should be ashamed of. Nobody said this quite that way. It was just the way it was.

Grandmother stayed in the hospital for a week, receiving treatment. Nobody ever told me what treatment she received. I assumed she received radiation treatment. It must have been awful. By this time, she was terribly crippled from her arthritis and had to be lifted to the toilet and could barely stand up. And everything about movement hurt. On top of this, her outlook was not good. I did not know this at the time, but she must have known. It was a time when I should have been extra nice, but I didn't know. How important it is to know.

While this was occurring, my grandfather was also showing signs of illness. He was becoming forgetful. He cashed a check for twenty-five dollars, which was a lot of money, and couldn't remember where he put it. He began to stutter and would try to find the right word. This was excused as old age. He was in his early to mid sixties. But he was getting worse, and nobody knew what to do about it. There was nothing that could be done.

He retired from the bank in my senior year and was not really happy being retired. He tried to open an office for business, but nothing came of that. Moreover, his salary was probably unchanged for several years, and his real retirement income was small. So he didn't have much money, unlike earlier years.

We had a careers day at my high school, and I thought he might be cheered up if he spoke to a group about careers in banking. He agreed to this, got dressed up, and made a good impression on everyone. In that moment, I believed that he had been cured and was on his way to recovery. In fact, he must have mustered all of his strength to make that presentation. The next day, his symptoms were back.

When I was sixteen years old, Grandfather came to me and asked to borrow a large amount of money, or it was large to me. He asked to borrow one thousand dollars. I had saved my money for years and had accumulated approximately one thousand two hundred dollars. I had mentioned this to Grandfather a few weeks before he asked for the loan. He also said I should keep quiet about the loan and not tell my grandmother or father. I did as he instructed and expected—just expected—to be repaid shortly.

Weeks went by, and there was no repayment. I told my grandmother, and she was upset. I began to listen to what was going on around Grandfather, and it didn't sound good. He had borrowed money on his rusty Ford car, and a man from the loan company came to our home, I gathered, to talk about repayment to the loan company. It became clear to me that Grandfather had overspent and had become deeply indebted. Maybe this was due to his advancing illness. Maybe it was due to inflation which had reduced his pension to a small amount of real income. Whatever it was, I wanted my money back and told him so. Then I asked again. He would avoid me when I asked this question, which was quite unlike him. After a while, I realized he had no way of repaying me. The money was gone.

Then about six months later, there was a stir in my grandmother's room, and my grandfather was there. His boyhood home, which had been vacant since my great-grandmother Pottinger had died, had burned to the ground. Weeks before, my grandfather had asked me if there was anything in the house that I wanted, and I asked for a picture of a lovely valley. It was an oil painting which I keep to this day. He gave me the picture, and that was about all that remained from the house.

A couple of months later, Grandfather repaid his loan to me. I assumed the money came from insurance on the house, but I never asked. Later, as I thought about the matter, I had certain questions in mind, but I never brought up the subject nor discussed the matter with anyone.

The extracurricular activities of high school were liberating, but the curriculum of courses was truly enlightening to me; I took all of the difficult courses and relished what I was learning—mathematics, history, English, the sciences—all were taught by knowledgeable teachers. They were willing to take time to tell all that they knew and what the frontiers of knowledge were like. Imagine that. High school teachers talking about who was the real Shakespeare, what mathematics would produce next, and what future foreign policy the United States would adopt out of necessity. We talked about these things every day. I have said many times that everything I use in daily life I learned in high school. People around me say they are embarrassed for me when they hear me say that, but it's true.

And it all came from what most people regarded as ordinary teachers. To me, they were far above the ordinary. They took the time to converse with me, advise me, and help me do what needed to be done. I suppose ordinary people do extraordinary things when they are patient and reach out to help others.

In my tenth grade, my gramma Smith had my mother arrange for a trip to visit relatives in Louisville, Kentucky. We were to visit cousins and spend a weekend. I didn't know we had these cousins and wondered why Mother placed so much importance on the trip. The pressure really came from Gramma Smith. So we took the New York Central train to Cincinnati and transferred to the Southern Railroad for the rest of the journey. Unlike my other Kentucky relatives, who were poor dirt farmers, these relatives were very prosperous and maybe rich. There was a big dinner, and I enjoyed the occasion. The next day, which was Saturday, we had breakfast, and the head of the house, Dr. Dare, asked me if I would like to join him during the day as he made rounds. I was delighted and put on a tie and jacket, so I would look as if I fitted into the scheme of things, whatever that might be. I learned that he was a doctor, but that was all I knew.

First, we went to the hospital, and he visited his patients. But before we went into their rooms, Dr. Dare took me aside in the hallway and quickly reviewed each patient. I didn't know much about what he said, but I knew a little. I was amazed that he took time to do this. He was obviously a busy man. Then he took me to his office where he reviewed results of tests. We did other things, and before long, a whole day had passed, and we returned to their home. The next day, we visited in the morning and then returned to our homes. On the train home, Gramma Smith asked me if I liked Dr. Dare and if I wanted to do what he did. I told her I liked him, but I hadn't given much thought to a medical career. I dropped the subject, and I forgot about it. But my mother didn't. Months later, she brought the subject up again and told me the reason for the trip was to let me know the family would be pleased if I would become a doctor, and Dr. Dare would find a way to make it possible. I didn't know any details, which I suppose could have been worked out. But I was flabbergasted. I had never thought Gramma Smith cared much about me. I thought for the first time about being a doctor and decided I should at least take all the science courses that were offered at Lakewood High School.

That meant courses in physics, chemistry, and biology during my final two years. The courses opened my mind to worlds I never dreamed existed. Biology was particularly fascinating. Here was the story of life, how it happened, how it sustained itself, and the beautifully logical way it was put together.

The result of all of this was that the Bausch and Lomb science award was given to me at graduation time. This is what all the science students hoped to get. Mr. Mahlon Povenmire, our principal, called me into his office to tell me the news. I didn't know what to say. I wasn't the smartest person in any of my science classes, and inside of me I knew I didn't deserve it. But what to do. I couldn't turn it down in any graceful way, so after the right words, which I stumbled over, I walked to the door. He stopped me and said that I would need to make another choice. I had also been nominated to receive what was called the departmental recipient in both social studies and science, and he said this was unusual to happen, and he felt I should choose between the two and that I should do so now because the announcement was about to be made.

Again I asked myself, how could this happen? A lot of very fine teachers were putting a great deal of confidence in me—that was all I could come up with. I chose the social studies award and felt terrible about disappointing my science teachers, who by now had become friends. As I walked back to my class, from where Mr. Povenmire had fetched me, I remembered Gramma Smith. She had made this beautiful dilemma, and how wonderful her inspiration had been and what it had led to.

Now all I had to do was face others who deserved these awards more than I—Gardner Weeks, Geof Paine, Dick Jacobs, Claude Rust, and several others. But nobody said anything, and I didn't share my worry with anybody except Jack Swanson, who said not to worry. He was right.

Mr. Povenmire also spoke to me about Deep Springs, and asked me if I would like to go there after graduation. My own thoughts were eastward to a college on the Atlantic coast. But I pursued the matter and found out that this school was deep in the California mountains, involved three years on a farm-and-school combination, paid for everything, and you finished your degree at Stanford University. It sounded very appealing, at least in abstract. Then my grandmother asked me how far away it was—three days on the train. In those days, nobody flew transcontinental, much less students. But I still persevered and went to visit an alumnus to hear the story from someone who had been there. This gentleman lived in Marion, which was two-hours' drive. He was not very impressive and lived in a sort of broken-down house. That did it for me. There was no Deep Springs in my future.

Yet I often think back about this, I presume, offer. It would have completely changed my life. I would have been a West Coast person through and through, with close friends in the Palo Alto area right from the beginning. But it would have meant also not seeing my family for three-quarters of a year at a time. All in all, I made the right choice to turn it down.

There was one experience in high school which was utterly sublime, and I will always cherish. That experience was to be director of the senior choir for half an hour.

Our high school had three choirs, a freshman choir, a junior choir, and a senior choir. So it was a singing school in every sense of the word. The senior choir had won a number of awards over the years and was the most ranking choir in northern Ohio. So the Fred Waring organization chose our senior choir to accompany them in a nationwide broadcast from Cleveland. At the time, Fred Waring had a large following. So he sent his rehearsal director to our high school to train us in a professional manner. Our regular director was Thelbert R. Evans, who was highly regarded. But the deal was that the Fred Waring director would do the job. This choir director was a genius. From the moment that he raised his hands, our choir sounded better. And as we practiced, we got better and better. I wondered what in the world he was doing that our regular director, Mr. Evans, wasn't doing. The concert was a great success, with lots of congratulations for all concerned.

Then came the day after with our regular choir rehearsal. Our choir was back in the dumps. The magic or whatever it was had evaporated. Things went along like this for a couple of weeks, and then there was a message during rehearsal for Mr. Evans to go to the office for some matter. He started to excuse himself, and then, in the stroke of the moment, asked me to keep the choir singing, as he put it, while he was away. That meant that I was to direct the choir.

I couldn't believe it. Why me? I was getting to do something I had always wanted to do. Maybe Mr. Evans sensed this. Anyway, on the way to the podium, I said to myself that we would go back to the wonderful sound of the Fred Waring conductor. I stood before the choir, took a deep breath, and raised my arms, and the music flowed. It would be inappropriate to say how well it all sounded, but afterward, a number of fellow choir members said that we sounded as good as we ever had been under the guest conductor. There was no question about how I felt. I was completely overwhelmed with joy. It remains today as a supreme moment. Maybe in my next life, I'll come back and do this.

Postscript

I graduated from high school in January 1952. That left nine months for me to work before I went to college. This was a busy time. I selected my college, worked as an adult for the first time, and traveled with two friends to the west of the country.

Selection of college was made easy. I applied for admission and scholarship to three colleges, Harvard, Yale, and Columbia. Harvard admitted me, but with no scholarship. Yale admitted me with no scholarship, but with a job in the dining halls that was not particularly difficult. Columbia admitted me with a scholarship. The decision was instantaneous. I would be off to Columbia in the fall. I would have preferred Yale, but the thought of a job didn't appeal to me, and I imagined that time on the job would be time off of studies or something else.

And it truly was not a disappointment. Columbia had programs that appealed to me very much and a faculty which was perhaps the best in the land. As I thought about it, I became more excited and happy about the turn of events. Best of all, one of my best friends, Jack Swanson, was going there one year ahead of me. And the Columbia young man two years my senior was Bruce Cook, who was Lakewood High's coolest person—just the coolest. Who wouldn't want to be associated with him.

So during the nine months between graduation from high school and freshman week at Columbia, I planned to look for a job. My chemistry teacher, Mr. Kluckhohn, suggested that I work in the laboratory of General Electric Company, which had a manufacturing plant on the east side of Cleveland. I was not enthused about spending all spring and summer inside a factory building. Even though this was one of the nicest factories around—it made light bulbs—it sounded a bit low level to me.

Instead, with my grandfather's help, I got a job as a new and used car salesman at Hull Dobbs, a Ford dealer located in downtown Cleveland. This job was an eye opener. It was a job with lots of practical experience in the business world. First of all, there were more characters than you could fit into a Broadway play. The sales manager was short, thin, nervous, and constantly walking fast to see someone. One of the salesmen, Maynard Joyner, was always busy with somebody and was never around when the dealer opened. Bob Erb was a consummate salesman—smooth, heavy, knew the right people to get credit approved, and was always chewing gum. The manager of the dealer was a hard-driving Southerner from Memphis, Tennessee, who kept reminding me that my grandfather had an obligation to find him a nice home to rent. Then there was Spunk Edmonds, an unreformed alcoholic who put on wildly hysterical demonstrations at the daily morning sales meetings of what went wrong the day before. I always liked Spunk and secretly admired his absolute independence, but I was sad at his lost battle with the bottle.

I managed to sell fourteen cars in this nine-month period, which gave me a little more money than I would have received from General Electric. But most of all, I realized that virtually all car sales depended on the customer being able to get a loan from a consumer credit company or a bank. Only one of my sales was for cash.

I learned that credit makes business happen. That was the most important lesson in business, and I was lucky to learn it early. Money makes the business world go round and round and round.

Jack Swanson, who was my good friend, and Dean Bowman, also a good friend and president of our class, and I piled into my dad's 1951 Ford Custom Tudor and headed for California. This was in August, so it was the hottest time of the year. But we had finished our summer jobs. We had three and a half weeks until college began, and California beckoned. That was a long way to drive, especially since the roads were all two-lane highways. The interstate system had been passed by Congress, but very little of it had been built. We saw all of the sights, and I even rode a donkey halfway down the Grand Canyon. Sometimes it was cold. It didn't matter to us.

We had a rollicking good time, especially when we stopped at one of Jack's fraternity houses. Jack was one year ahead of Dean and myself and had already joined the Sigma Chi fraternity, which was always known for good living, good fun, and keeping on the good side of the college dean. But the trip was primarily one of vistas and sights. The most impressive to me was the view of Lake Tahoe, coming over the Sierra mountains. Only the view of Yosemite comes close to the grandeur of that moment.

Chapter 6
Alma Mater
1952 to 1956

After I arrived, I never felt comfortable at Columbia College, which is the college of Columbia University. There was a vast difference from high school, where I fitted in, and there was a common culture. At Columbia, I felt like a stranger.

I realized that this was to be a broadening experience, and it was. But this college was different in a fundamental way. Most of my fellow students were commuters. They would arrive at nine o'clock, go to classes, and then leave by four o'clock, returning to their homes.

The students also lived on another wave length. They mostly came from first- or second-generation immigrants whose mothers, particularly, were motivating them to excel and study. All of this creates the most competitive and hardworking, scholarly community imaginable.

On top of that, most of the class was headed for medical school. In those days, this was the one job that assured you of a very comfortable living and a high standing in the community. This college of 641 freshmen, where 460 students graduated four years later, provided one in sixty-nine doctors to America. Nobody liked to talk about it, but it was a doctor mill.

Of course, Columbia College was this and more, much more. But the premeds set the pace. Everyone else followed.

I felt college should be a place where you would learn the skills of a gentleman. Specialized schools where you learn a trade or skill, such as medicine, accounting, or landscape horticulture, are for another time and place. There is not much disagreement on this.

But the experience of college should also be like going to a duke's court in Italy or a court in England in the olden days. There you made friends for life, learned courtesy and manners, and acquired that polish which sets gentlemen and ladies apart from the ordinary and rough.

The best colleges do this, and that is why we respect and admire them. I realize that this view is not appreciated by most people, but that's all right.

What to do. By Thanksgiving in my freshman year, I decided that it would take all of my time and resources just to have a respectable class standing. It would be on this basis that I would have the best chance of being admitted to law school. Just as the premeds used the college as the springboard to medicine, I would use the college to the best law school.

At the time, Harvard was the highest esteemed school, but I kept hearing that Yale was the best to attend, because they were least purely legal and incorporated social sciences into their training. I liked that. I was somewhat intimidated by the legalese approach that I sensed law school required. I knew my family, especially my dad and grandfather, pinned their hopes on my achieving this goal.

Thus, in a strange way, I was like those commuters. We were all trying to do our best to get out of a trap. I wanted to soar and not be scared about keeping a job or doing something that was dull, working deep inside the basement of a company. We all wanted to escape from the ordinary and being poor.

I did not join a fraternity, and I suppose that led to my being on the outside. I was close to two frat houses, Sigma Chi and Delta Psi, but that wasn't the same as being a member of the house.

So I tried to organize events on my own. I tried to put together a dining group, but it fizzled out. I did succeed in organizing a class dinner in my junior year, and about eighty classmates attended. Several friends asked me if I planned to run for class president afterward. I declined. In retrospect, I probably should have done so. How could it have hurt?

Despite my scholarship and summer earnings, there was still a need for money to pay the bills. My father was always very generous and made sure that I was never short of money. During my freshman year, total expenses, including tuition of six hundred dollars, was one thousand eight hundred dollars. The tuition was covered by a scholarship. I lived very well on this amount. Several friends lived on fifteen to sixteen hundred dollars, and that was a squeeze for them. The generosity of my father continued throughout my years of study. I wish that I had expressed my gratitude more often.

During my first semester, I lived in Hartley Hall, a college dormitory. I had two roommates, Stu Glass and David Goler. Stu took me under his wing and introduced me to Jewish life in New York. It was a wonderful experience. He took me to temple, entertained me in his home, and his friends accepted me as a long-lost member. David sat in his chair and never said a word.

In the rest of college, I had my own room in John Jay Hall, a more modern dormitory. My neighbors were Bob Long, Neil Klein, and Chet Forte. Chet was the star of the basketball team, although he was short, about five feet nine inches tall. The hall was always filled with basketball players, all good people. Neil was quiet and a good friend.

Bob became a life-long friend, and we shared many college experiences. I will always thank him for literally pulling me to hear Mark Van Doren lecture. I never heard such an outstanding lecturer. His subject was English and other literature. He made things simple and gave us the impression that he was discovering new ideas right on the spot before the class. It was really an act, or I should say he was a great actor. I have come to believe that in any field, to be a leader you must first be a consummate actor.

Most meals were bought in local sandwich shops or dingy diners and restaurants. One of these was Aki's, a Chinese restaurant that gave you a three-course dinner for ninety-nine cents. The food was about what you would expect it to be.

The dean of the college, Neil Chamberlain, asked me to visit him from time to time, and I did so. During these meetings, I would talk about everything under the sun. He was a cool man, never upset, with a rational answer for everything. I liked him and admired him, and he was, like me, from the Midwest. I never understood why he wanted me to visit him, and I regarded this to be a special privilege none of my friends had. I suspect he held out great hopes for me, and I realize this was a bit presumptuous to think. But whatever the reason, it was a fine experience.

In contrast to Dean Chamberlain, there was Dean McKnight, with the title of Dean of Students. Dean McKnight was number two dean. I never liked him. I thought he was a class-one windbag. He was always harrumphing and clearing his throat, smoking a half-lighted cigar, looking down at whomever he was speaking to, and pronouncing forth words in a thick New York accent. I always went out of my way to avoid him. But I suppose I was way too harsh. He was, I am sure, actually a kindly man. Underneath the veneer, I think he had a warm heart.

It was just my prejudice against what I felt was the New York influence. I felt culturally superior, being from the Midwest. It was hard to take New Yorkers as equals. We in the Midwest made everything that people used, or so I thought, and New Yorkers were stuffed shirts. I actually believed that, and how wrong it was.

One person who kept my spirits up and was a great booster for Columbia was Maurice C. Hull, who lived in Cleveland.

He was a charmer, and his wife, Bertha, was as gracious as a duchess. Mr. Hull saw all of the good things in everything, and he made you feel like you were on top of the world when you parted ways. He was a master salesman for a typewriter company, and he attended the college in the early 1920s. I am eternally grateful to him, probably for my scholarship, and also his enthusiasm and positive attitude toward Columbia. He showed me how important attitude was in life. May his spirit live on.

I was a philosophy major, but I'm not sure what that means. I liked the clarity of thinking that philosophy demanded, and its abstraction seemed so clever. But philosophy in my years at college lacked a personal touch, and it was remote from the day-to-day life of earning a living. My dad picked this up and had several talks with me about it. He wanted me to take an accounting course. It seemed so remote and difficult to understand, so I put his suggestion aside. But he made his point, and I began to look around for something else.

My advisor was Henry Graff, a New Yorker with a smile. I got along with him, but he didn't do any real advising. But as luck would have it, in the next office was Bob Carey, who was professor of economics. I was walking by his door one day, saw him, and he saw me, and we struck up a conversation. That led to other times together, and I found my mentor. Professor Carey was from Stockton, California, went to the University of the Pacific, and had all of the bounce and good humor that I enjoyed.

Then in my junior year, Bob Carey asked me if I would like to join his seminar in economics, which was a reading of the great books of economics throughout history. He told me not to worry that I didn't take the introductory course or any other course in economics. In that course and through Bob Carey's eyes, I saw the whole perspective of economics thought, not just the current vogue that was the way of Lord Keynes, which was taught as doctrine in the preliminary courses at the time.

I was enthusiastic about that seminar, and for the first time, realized I should become an economist. It was the study of how the business of the world functioned. I was overwhelmed by the power of the ideas. This was power to create and power to destroy. What a privilege to have this knowledge. What a perspective to have in one's possession.

This was a time when economists were hardly known. Virtually nobody knew what they did. Yet it was clear to me that they would be important in the future, because they held the keys to understanding how the goals of a society and individual businesses and each person could be fulfilled. It also explained how wealth was created, both for a nation and for individual people. Imagine the secrets—or what until now had been not understood and not known—of doing things in a way that could make you rich. At the very least, it could take you out of poverty. No other study could do these things. That knowledge somebody would consider worthwhile. Why wouldn't I want to find out these things?

Prof. Carey and I talked about these things, and it all led to his encouragement of me to do more work in economics, even though he knew of my intent to go to law school. He seemed to think that there would be time to carry on in economics. He also held out as the finest use of economics to be teaching. I realized that he was a teacher, and in a way, he was talking about himself. But in a more profound way, he was right. Teaching is probably the most elevated occupation of all. It shares knowledge with others and multiplies one's larger contribution to many others. To have knowledge and not to share it is unforgivable selfishness.

So I entered Prof. Carey's seminar of great books in economics. This was a senior course and was supposed to be the capstone to three years of economics courses. The good professor told me not to worry but to dig in. The amazing thing about economics for me is that I never took the introductory course. Rather, I read the ideas of economics in their original form, so I knew what the thinkers in the field really meant, not what some intermediary might want me to think.

It was in this great books seminar that I formulated my thinking about free markets and how they were the basis of the best in economics. This is where I concluded that there were no good objections or exceptions to this. All sound economics would be built on this foundation. That simple principle served me well in the course of the years that were to come, and it also got me into a lot of trouble.

Professor Carey had an enormous positive impact on my life, as future events revealed. It was worth four years at Columbia just to meet him.

My grades were respectable, *B* plus for an overall average. My junior year was my best year, and I did study intently that year. During my sophomore summer, I read Arnold Toynbee's *A Study of History*, which opened my eyes to the grandeur of knowledge. One of his ideas was that there are repeating cycles in history, which I found adaptable to economics. It was a heady experience.

I even won a prize, much to my surprise. It was for the outstanding student in the great books course, which is required of all freshmen. The prize was the Kinney Prize, and it consisted of a certificate and a book. I regret to say I don't know where that book went. I didn't feel that I had done anything special and actually received a *B* plus grade for the course. Many others received higher grades of *A* minus, and there were actually two straight *A*'s. But as Professor Hyman Klieman said it, he had seldom seen such passion for the literature, and he spoke of how this intensity of mine spread to many others. I was a bit embarrassed, since I knew that others had just as much passion and were a lot smarter and understood the books better.

But I accepted the prize gracefully and then forgot about it.

The interest in economics was along the side of applying to law school, which I did to Yale. It was the only place that I applied in November, which was a bit of unwarranted pride. Anyway, I was admitted in January.

As if to celebrate, I did something extravagant—I took a three-week vacation in Cuba. This was just before Fidel Castro came to power, and there were rumblings that this was going to happen.

But my trip was pure vacation. I told myself that I had worked hard and now could take time off. This thinking I now realize was plain rubbish. I didn't deserve anything of the sort.

The trip was not a hit with my family, especially when I asked them for some money to tide me over until I returned to school. But for all of that flack, it was worth it. I had the time of my life and traveled into the interior of the island, to Caibarrien, Santa Clara, and the city of Trinidad. Fidel Castro took over the island six months later, and I was surprised at that. People were not dissatisfied, and what happened was a mystery to me. I think a small well-organized group knew what to do. It made me feel that freedom is precarious.

My hotel bills were seldom more than fifty cents a night; food was cheap. I was treated like a visiting dignitary, and in one place, they held a school assembly in my honor—the assembly featured a piano selection and dances. I applauded, bowed, and gave flowers to the performers.

I behaved like visiting royalty and never have quite got over this highly preferential treatment. The city of Trinidad was filled with gorgeous but dilapidated old colonial homes, which someday, after Cuba opens up, will be restored and form the basis of a magnificent resort city. The beaches were beautiful. Havana had throb and beat of a Latin city, as people literally lived in the streets. It was a great experience, which I was to pass on to Sylvi.

Graduation week, like freshman week, was a time of high spirits. And graduation ceremonies finally arrived. Both my father and mother came to New York to see this event.

There were two ceremonies. One was for all university graduates, which my father wanted to see, but I, quite wrongly, declined. The second was for the college. That was the one that I felt an affinity toward. It unfortunately involved a mishap which should not have happened.

My mother stayed at the King's Crown Hotel, which was half a block away from the college ceremonies. She didn't know where the ceremonies would be held, so she asked me to ask my father to come and get her and take her to the event. I passed this on to my father, and he agreed. I actually mentioned this twice more, since I didn't want a slip up. Well, my father never arrived, and my mother missed the ceremony. She was really upset; in fact, she had a fit. I always felt my dad had no intention of escorting Mother to the graduation, a sort of punishment to her.

This cast a sad cloud over the day. I remember looking out at the families that accompanied their sons. For a moment, I resented my situation with divorced parents. But not for long. There just wasn't room in my life to harbor resentment. It is a broken way of living. There is too much to do, and there is too much of a need for energy for me to get bogged down in that. Let the chips fall where they may, and get on with things.

I always had a summer job. Each was different, and all were interesting.

For example, one summer I was an assistant to an airport lighting engineer. I was completely a gopher, but I learned how many aspects there were to lenses and intensities of light and carried away a new appreciation of light.

One job had a humorous moment I'll never forget. It had to do with the Cook Coffee Company. A friend had a friend, Mr. Reeder, who was the dispatcher for Cook's delivery trucks. These were like the panel vans that are used today. We were the summer crew that took over the routes of the delivery salesmen during their vacations. I say "we" because I got my friend Jack Swanson a job with the company as well as one for myself. The customers were housewives.

Well, it got humid and hot in August, and I decided to wear shorts to make my rounds. One—or maybe more—of the good ladies called Mr. Reeder, the dispatcher boss, and complained that her deliveryman was wearing shorts. Mr. Reeder interpreted this to mean shorts as in underwear shorts. I, of course, was wearing Bermuda shorts, which were just then coming into style. When I saw him, as I was loading the truck the next morning, he called me into his office for a little talk about dress codes. We both had a good laugh when I explained it all. But he still said to keep the Bermuda shorts at home.

Chapter 7
New Course
1957

The first week, I knew I was at the wrong place. New Haven was a small town and much quieter than New York. My classmates were the best people you could find anyplace, anytime. But studying law was not what I was cut out to do.

The whole idea of using past decisions as the basis for current life was not how I am put together. I know the reasons this can make sense for society, and I know how this way of handling the law developed through the ages. And I am grateful that we have a legal system based on the accumulated wisdom of many centuries. Not to mention that our freedoms are based on the ability of one single individual being able to challenge the totality of government—at least theoretically.

But this was for someone else. I knew that I should be back in economics. The question was how to do it. The task was complicated by a surprise visit by my father, grandmother, and grandfather the weekend of the law school's social weekend. It wasn't the time—in fact, there was no time—to talk.

So at the end of the semester, I transferred back to Columbia and entered their graduate school of arts and sciences in the economics department. I spoke with Professor Carey, and he welcomed me, set me up with Carter Goodrich (an eminent economic historian—just the person I wanted), and even arranged for a scholarship to take care of tuition.

I told everybody at home after it was all done. At first, they were disappointed but, after a short time, simply said that I should study what I wanted. My father took the news on an upbeat note. My grandmother was sad. I think she wanted me, most of all, to become a lawyer like my grandfather.

With my grandfather, it was a different kind of story. He had been failing in health for the previous five years. His mind was deteriorating, and he had begun to lose weight. He had put on quite a bit of weight when he was middle-aged, and at this time, that was gone; and he was thin, perhaps too thin. We now recognize this as Alzheimer's disease, but at the time, it was simply regarded as hardening of the arteries. He really didn't grasp what was going on. The task of looking after him fell on my father's shoulders, which he accepted gracefully and completely.

So at this time, my father was a caretaker for both of his parents, as well as working to keep income flowing. My grandfather had a small pension from the Cleveland Trust Bank, but it didn't amount to much. And surprisingly, I was to learn years later, he was still paying off a debt to something called the Mapes Estate for some money he had borrowed to buy stock in 1929.

Chapter 8
Graduate School of Economics
1957 to 1958

I was now in graduate school studying what I would be doing for the rest of my life. I had a lot of catching up to do. There were major areas I had only a light background in my knowledge, such as the all-important theory course, which was and still is the important core of economics—and which was to be an important issue in graduate school here and abroad—as well as later in the working world.

And there were key other areas where I needed to acquire proficiency, including accounting and especially statistics. I was amazed at statistics, what it could tell you. It is the language of economics and a new way of seeing virtually everything. My life was not the same after that statistics course.

There were other courses which were not so basic, but still important. One was in public finance taught by Lowell Harris, whom I knew from the college. It helped to have the college connection. It was as if I were in one big family. In fact, the graduate faculties were a friendly and very open place to study. Columbia's senior division of the university is absolutely the finest, and I was happy to be there.

The theory course was taught by William Vickery, who was a maverick. He had literally translated all of traditional theory of supply and demand into indifference curves. What this meant, from a practical point of view, was that I had to learn theory twice. And then I had to learn the Keynesian theory, which was the rage in economics at that time. This theory promised to keep an economy on an improving trend for as far as could be seen. Professor Vickery later won the Nobel Prize in economics and was brilliant beyond measure. What an opportunity to study with such a person.

But to tell the truth, I was always trying to figure out what he was saying. So I had to study theory largely on my own behalf. And this was good, because I had to figure out each step and prove to myself what was declared as a fact.

And it came as a great surprise, as I was doing this, that what was accepted as fact was in fact not a fact. In essence, the whole basis of theory, as it was being taught, had not been proven and, as best as I could see, was inaccurate and wrong as well. It turned out to be a challenge to me in that it did not fit into academia at the time.

In essence, what I observed was that countries with the slowest recovery from the Second World War—like Britain— had the most central planning and an economy largely driven by a central bank. Debt, not equity capital, was the engine for growth. Precisely, the reverse was true with the economies that were springing ahead, such as Germany. Yet Keynesian theory preached that the role of a central bank would be the right answer for expansion. It was all wrong. But that was what we were supposed to learn and, God forbid, possibly practice someday, if we ever went to work for the Federal Reserve Bank.

All of this was what I wanted to say to my advisor, Carter Goodrich, who listened with bemused interest. I thought he was interested, in a way, from his economic history perspective. Still, there was no fire for the idea.

Carl Shoup was head of the Department. He was a bit remote from me, possibly because I did not take one of his courses in finance.

Then there was Arthur Burns, former chairman of the Federal Reserve, who taught business cycles. Burns was a great showman. He often played erudite games with his class. In one instance, he was challenged by a wunderkind from Brooklyn, who also took a course in business cycles from City College of New York. Burns led him on and on down a path that he chose. Then in the final five minutes, utterly demolished this poor fellow's position. Burns did this sort of thing often. It was entertaining, but I don't think it was good teaching. I know that in my case I didn't say much in class out of fear that I too would be caught in his quicksand.

During this period, my roommate was Paul Levine, a friend from college days. We rented a large apartment on 116th Street. It was a bargain at the time, although I forgot exactly what we paid. The apartment was handed down to us by Jim Barker and Tony Barber, who had repaired whatever damage they did to it, so it was in pretty good condition when we moved in. Alas, we were too quiet to do much new damage.

About this time, my grandmother on my father's side of the family became ill again. She went to the Cleveland Clinic for treatment with X-rays. Nobody said it, but she had throat cancer. The treatment left her weak. I felt very sorry for her. Yet we never talked about it. I never knew how she felt about it day to day. Or how she felt about the future, living with cancer.

That was the way it was. Everybody pretended nothing had happened. And I was busy with my own situation, so I didn't give the matter a lot of thought. I am sorry about this. At least my aunt Ethel, grandmother's sister, came to our home for several months to look after grandmother, and that was good.

As I recall those times, I realize how self-centered I must have been. And I wish that I could live some of those hours over again, so I could help and serve those who had helped me. My father always had tucked in the back of his mind a little saying that reminded him that we should always be as pleasant and helpful as possible, because we can't live today twice—and we should never have regrets. He said it better than that, but the message is there. I know that I deeply wish that I could have an hour—or even a few minutes—a few moments—to have the loved ones of my life, to be present with them and tell them how much they mean to me, even after all these years.

I must not have been a compassionate person at this time

of my life. Even though I probably have forgotten many of the misdeeds—as well as let many deeds slip in my memory—I still feel uneasy about this period. One small incident just now comes to mind. Our next-door neighbors, Mr. and Mrs. Norman Bill, were selling their home and 1950 Oldsmobile four-door sedan, and I had told them if they sold the car, I would like to buy it. Well, the moment arrived. They wanted three hundred fifty dollars for it, and I didn't have the money, and I already had a car. So I declined to buy it. They were very disappointed. And I was embarrassed. But I wasn't myself, and I didn't offer to help them sell the car, and I was abrupt. I remember the occasion with sadness and regret. It seems like a little thing now, but life is made up of little things, and in fact, all the little things are bigger than the big things. I would give anything to have that occasion to live over. Perhaps this is how we learn. I hope so.

During these years, I spent a lot of time at the home of John and Dick Albright. John followed me to Columbia, and his younger brother Dick went to Yale. John was the most loyal of friends and was with me through thick and thin. His mother treated me like one of her own sons.

There were many hilarious moments and a sad one. John and Dick lost their father at this time. He was a good-natured, fun-loving dad. In any situation, he would egg me on. One time, a religious group tried to be sure we were saved. I pretended not to be, and they gave me the full treatment. There was no place to hide. Only a confession would do. I was humbled, and the visitors walked away triumphant. All of this took place on their front porch. And so it went. Day in and day out, there were lots of pranks. The whole family was usually in attendance, including grandparents. All were very alert and ready to laugh.

Mr. Hull, who was the Cleveland man for Columbia, suggested that in addition to my graduate studies there, I might wish to study at Oxford, England. My studies at Columbia would give me a master's degree. The Oxford idea would be a side track for a doctorate, but Mr. Hull felt the broadening experience of perhaps the finest university of all should be considered. By this time, Mr. Hull had become my senior advisor, in effect, so I took seriously any suggestion he made. To cap it all off, he helped me apply for and receive a Huntington scholarship, which is an award from the estate of one of John D. Rockefeller's close associates. I also received a scholarship to the University of Cologne in Germany, which I was unable to accept, but not without a lot of soul searching.

And I did apply and was admitted to Corpus Christi College to read for a master's degree. At the time, Oxford did not offer a higher degree in economics.

To complete my Columbia master's degree, I wrote a thesis titled, "Research in the Petroleum Industry." This was not one of my shining achievements. It was an interesting subject at the time, but to this day, I can't remember one thing about it. The dissertation was accepted by some committee, and it fulfilled my requirement to have done the work. I never like to do things that are not the best I can do and are directed to something important, but it happened this time.

Chapter 9
Oxford
1958 to 1960

The two years at Oxford were sublime. Oxford is the finest place to study. And the outstanding friends that welcomed me to Corpus Christi College, where I studied, have endured a lifetime.

I got to Oxford traveling across the Atlantic ocean on the Dutch ship *Maasdam*, a small liner that took eight days. I loved the days at sea, although the ship was nothing special. It was, in fact, a bit spartan. I was on it because the ship I was scheduled to sail on, the *United States*, was on strike. That was the premier ship of the seas.

Once in England, at Southampton, I took a train to Oxford—one of those small coal-burning trains you see in the old English movies that never went faster than thirty-five miles per hour.

My lodgings were in a rooming house run by the college, and my room was small, cold in the winter, with a hearty breakfast. I soon got used to ample breakfasts, because they were the best meal of the day. The rest of the food at the college and in England left a lot to be desired. But after a while, I got used to it. That is until I traveled to France and tasted beans the way nobody else can make them.

England had still not recovered from the Second World War, which ended thirteen years earlier. There were still shortages of anything special. Clothes rationing had recently ended.

The hours during the day were spent in the beautiful library of the college and in a racing boat on the Isis River. This is really the Thames River, but upstream, it has this different name.

When I was in residence at the university, I was considered to be "up." That was the term that was used to say that you were in residence. Oxford University was the umbrella university for twenty-three colleges. The colleges were where everything happened. Corpus was the smallest of these colleges, which was a great advantage in that I was able to know almost all of the members of the college. Corpus was also a scholarly college, but not too much so, which meant books were important, but sports were too. It was a college of all-round excellence, but nothing showy.

The reason Oxford is such a fine place for knowledge is the tutorial system. Cambridge also uses this way of education and is probably just as good at its task, but as the saying goes, Oxford is more interesting news.

Tutorials are simply one-on-one discussions between a faculty member, or a "don," and a student. Usually, the student also writes a short paper, which is read at the tutorial. Meetings are usually once a week but sometimes are twice a week.

The usual university system of teaching is the lecture. Here, a professor or lecturer expounds on a subject, and there is not the intense scrutiny that is typical of the tutorial. The lecture is typically quite boring, while the tutorial is virtually always a lively conversation.

The sad part of these years was that in the winter of my first year, my grandmother died back in Lakewood. She had been failing the summer before I left. She had lost weight and was struggling even more in her almost completely paralyzed state. Arthritis is such a terrible affliction, and she knew no time out but was reminded every waking moment of being immobile and in unending pain. I often would forget this because she never complained. I believe she died from the spreading of her cancer from her throat, but I never discussed her final time with anybody. I just didn't want to know the details. She was gone, and that was that.

I never thought that when I left her earlier that year in September, I would not see her again. The thought never occurred to me. And being across an ocean at a time when transatlantic travel was still by boat meant it would be almost impossible to return to the States for her funeral. Maybe I didn't want to face the heartbreak. Yet the loss of not being there, at her end, still hurts as it comes to mind.

Her last letter to me trailed off, as her writing became a simple line, and then stopped. I was told by this what was going to happen, but I still didn't want to believe it. Christmas must have been bleak at home. But my father never let on how he felt. I knew the house would be empty.

As much as I could fathom, all of Oxford's economics dons and university professors were dyed in the wool Keynesians. By this time, I had formed strong opinions about this system of economics—that it was the wrong way to run an economy, and it didn't really work.

This led to lively and, at times, heated discussions. I felt that I had the facts on my side, but the dons had the weight of the university on their side. It was all for the good, until examinations rolled around. At that time, I felt myself caught between my convictions and fulfilling my academic requirements, but that came later. In the meantime, I was having the time of my life.

The socialism of the time was voted in by the electorate. The British people got what they wanted. The leaders couldn't be faulted for fulfilling the requests of the popular demands. And socialism was quite popular. Or I should say, given the lame alternatives which were presented, socialism appeared to look pretty good. It would be three and a half decades before Margaret Thatcher presented a viable alternative to socialism.

In addition to politics, the requirement was to study philosophy. At first, I couldn't see the need for this, but once into the subject, it became clear. No program can go anywhere without knowing what it is all about. Philosophy has that core thinking which is essential to anything that is well done.

Neville Ward Perkins was my economics don. He was

a resident of Pembroke College. I was fortunate to have this brilliant and wise tutor. We got along famously, and he was, as he would say, "tolerant" of my ideas, as he would shove the doctrine of Keynes before me. Another American, Dan Arnow, and I would often be his guests at his home in the beautiful Cotswalds countryside to pick apples or do yard work he set aside for us. And which we did gladly.

Some of the best moments were when we sat around a roaring fire, and he told us stories of his work in the war cabinet of Winston Churchill. The Prime Minister had set up a special small group that reported to the war cabinet, which was charged with the mission of figuring out a plan to win the war. This was in 1940, when it seemed that nothing could stop the Wehrmacht. The group took its task seriously and came up with a plan. Britain would keep up the fight and produce what was needed for current requirements, while the commonwealth, such as Canada and Australia and other like countries, would produce an increasing surplus.

In simple terms, the war would be fought like the one with Napoleon. Gradually the continental forces would face declining output, would make more than a few colossal mistakes, and would collapse from within. That was the fate of Napoleon. Ward Perkins was full of stories like this and never failed to rivet my attention. Sadly, he died a month before my examinations, and I lost a deeply felt friend and, as it turned out, an ally when I really needed one.

Michael Brock was dean of the college, and he also was

one of my tutors in British political history when I first arrived. This material provided the background to the economics of the times over the past two hundred years. As a don, Brock was outstanding. It all made sense, the advent of socialism with that background. Socialism is still a terrible economic system, defeating the very objectives of improved welfare of the people and a more civilized workplace. But the tutorials made it clear and reasonable the way that it happened in Britain. We continue to be good friends and have enjoyed visits with Michael Brock and his most charming wife, Eleanore.

At that time, sports was a gentlemanly activity. You played the game. You tried to win. The game was over. And you got together at a pub to celebrate. How different this was from the American attitude of success at all costs. The Oxford approach could be quite focused and serious, if the contest was important like the Oxford versus Cambridge rowing race. Then the best of the rowers trained at precision timing and were the best in the world.

Everyone at Corpus played a sport, or almost everyone. I had no plans of playing anything and was in the library one splendid September day when two rowing members came up to me and made it clear that I had an obligation to come down to the river and get into a skull and to begin practice right there and now. Such friendly pressure was irresistible. Up on the bow of this thin and fast boat was Keith Kirkman, a short and stout fellow from South Africa, who barked out orders. Our boat did its best and from that time on I was on the crew team.

Everything else was handled in the same manner. Great

courtesy and an eye out for good fellowship. People counted, their feelings always had to be considered. It was the way it was.

I became friends with an outstanding group, informally headed by Ed Johnson. Ed was a hale and hearty fellow who was—and is—the kindest of gentleman. His sport was hockey, and we took a trip to Spain with his team, visiting local clubs as well as Ian Mackenzie's home on top of a hill overlooking his father's copper mines. We were a bit too high in spirit and downed some of his father's best spirits—a special very old brandy. His father was not happy about that. But that is how it went; bouncing along dictator Franco's still destroyed Spain. It was like England of the old days, of the time before the First World War, when being British meant you ran the world.

Only times had changed. My studies showed that Britain was not keeping up with exports but was covering the gap by government sales of oil from the Mideast. This was before the great American exploration and development in Saudi Arabia. As I looked at these figures and looked at many areas that had been damaged in London and still not repaired, my feelings went out to these people who won the challenge of freedom and were still waiting for its economic rewards.

One friend felt this very deeply, and that was Brian Sedgemore. He was a dyed-in-the-wool conservative at Oxford but remarkably changed alliance to become a Labor party member and went on to become a member of Parliament and a member of several Labor governments. He was a big man with a voice that could be heard around the island, and he was a loyal friend.

Not everyone was a top person, as the phrase went. One person whom I brushed shoulders with was Richard Gott. This diminutive member of the college turned out to be a traitor to Britain. He was a Russian spy. I was always polite to him, but there was something about him that made me want to keep my distance. His personality told it all. What a terrible thing to be mixed up with.

Ed Johnson was the undesignated leader of our group. He kept information flowing, everything up to the minute of what was happening to so-and-so and who should hurry to do this or that. He was our shepherd. And the place where we would usually end up was the Bear, which was a pub down a walled narrow street, just a hundred steps from the center of the college, where a graceful pelican held sway over the courtyard. Here there was a welcome for everybody, and the scrapes and difficulties were soon swept away with a pint or two or three. Pubs are a true English way of getting together and a place where friendship means loyalty. The libation helps, but only seldom does someone overindulge, and then that poor devil is transported one way or another to his nightly resting place. It is all so civilized, so basic, and so human.

At the Bear, an honor was bestowed on me, which I regrettably did not accept. The pub master asked if I would like my tie to be placed in a special case. This meant cutting the tie in half. I liked the tie and declined. That was a mistake. It would still be there if I had agreed. And a bit of me would have remained in that little hole in the stone wall. The tie is now long gone, just the way things go.

One of the great advantages of Oxford is the time for travel and reading. This was as important as the tutorials. The trip to Spain, which was then ruled by the dictator Franco, opened my eyes to what a dictator does to the people as well as the economy. He impoverishes both.

On the lighter side, there was travel to places all over Europe. Vienna was for Christmas, and Rome was for Easter. While in Rome, I bought a motor scooter, a Lambretta TV 175, blue-green and white, with license plate number Roma 191413. It was a gleaming vehicle. When the weather was cold, it was very cold on this machine. But there will be no sight as beautiful as a field of flowers coming into Florence on a fine spring day following a rain the night before. I rode it everywhere, and it never failed me. It was a sad day when I sold it in Denmark, just before I returned to the United States.

Following the war, of all the arts in Vienna, music was first to be revived. The concert hall was rebuilt within a year of the time the country became free. It was painted white inside with gold leaf trim and brilliant crystal chandeliers everywhere. During intermission, the men and women walked in a circle, like a promenade. Everyone had a new suit or dress and looked terrific. No casual clothes here.

Paris showed off everything and also was a mecca for food. You could eat better for less than anywhere else except Austria.

That meant something. Students are the last to be considered in the food department.

During the summer of my two-year stay, I went to a small village in Austria to study German. That seemed to be the best combination of pleasure and something that could be accomplished. The place was Mayerhofen, near Innsbruck, right in the middle of the Alps. It was a beautiful village, full of spring flowers in the middle of the summer. My German came along nicely, and it turned out I could actually carry on a conversation from what I learned.

One of the attendees, also an American, was Sally Orcutt, from Wellesley, near Boston. We did lots of things together, including an excursion up the trail to a lookout point that showed what seemed like the whole world below us. Sally was always ready to go—to do whatever seemed to be right for the moment. She met me, with my father and a cousin, June, in New York City, when I returned, and also moved to Palo Alto; and our paths still cross from time to time. When we first moved to Palo Alto, she invited me to a party and brought out some old photographs of us. Maie was not bemused.

Yet there was a certain edge to life at Oxford in the late fifties. These young men had grown up hearing the tales of valor in two great wars, one just finished. And there was nothing like holding fast to the principles of civilization in the face of barbarous warfare. The Germans were seen as Lord Asquith, prime minister during the first war with Germany, said, "Brutes they are and brutes they remain." I casually mentioned this quote on a number of occasions, expecting it to be one of those immediately discarded pieces of conversation, but in every instance, the English person to whom I was talking was struck by the quote and took a moment to ponder—to let the enormity of what was said sink in. Nothing like that would ever happen at Columbia University.

When all of this was discussed, very delicately, with students in Germany, a different story emerged. Many of them saw the role of Germany as protecting the culture and civilization of the West against the barbarous Soviet onslaught from the east and felt that the Soviet threat was what was important. They even regretted the war with England as being unfortunate and need not have happened if England had stayed neutral.

Of course, there were two tyrannies; each worse than the other, if that would be possible. Fairness and freedom know no apologies. There can be no compromise and still keep them flying high.

All of this set me up as appearing to be a representative of a now-supremely powerful nation that was mindless of its mission. There was consternation at me, I felt, because I would someway inherit this power that recently was Britain's, and I would not understand its mission in preserving the individual recognition for it all. I was, in short, regarded as a somewhat mindless giant.

One member of the college who felt this very much was Tim Mitford, who had served as an officer in the Royal Navy. The navy in England is regarded as the "senior service," and the ultimate guardian of England's heritage. Tim always was friendly, but there was a certain bite to his thoughts. I liked Tim and admired what he stood for. Tim never realized this.

In the final months of my first year at Corpus, I received a letter from Carl Shoup, who was chairman of the Columbia Graduate Faculty of Economics. He urged me to return to Columbia to continue my work toward a doctorate and to leave Oxford. There was no question that I wanted to stay two years at Oxford to receive my master's degree, but I felt from the tone of the letter that he would not look with pleasure on this. I wanted to finish both degrees.

Yet I had worn myself out with universities and wanted, sooner rather than later, to get out into the world of affairs, find my job, and live like people did everywhere on a day-to-day basis. I never replied to the letter. I didn't know what to say. So on my next trip to New York City, I plan to go to the Columbia economics department and bring up the subject. Somehow, this area of my life was never finished.

I had a half-baked solution to this at the time. I dreamed up an idea of attending the University of Rotterdam to continue the doctorate. I even applied for a Marshall scholarship and received a scholarship from these people, although not a full-fledged Marshall. Still, it would have been enough money to commute twice a month to Rotterdam and pursue a doctorate from the University of Rotterdam. Of course, this could exist only in the air, and it wasn't realistic. I also got myself into trouble with the officialdom that ran the program, I think, when I turned it down in the fall. In all, I wasn't at my best.

Instead of commuting to Rotterdam, I was doing much more pleasant things. One was to visit a friend, Philip Crofton, with his family during a festival weekend at his public (really private) school.

In the late afternoon, it was the custom for all members of the college to assemble in the junior commons room. Here, for about half of an hour, everybody saw everybody else and shared the talk of the times. There was lots of laughter, a few pints of beer, and we would then attend dinner in the dining hall, with its pictures of former great men who had sat in the same seats. One of these translated the bible into plain English, so that the common man could read scripture for himself, much as Martin Luther did for the German people. Forever afterward, no central authority could squelch the most sacred religious document of all. The gifts to England, as reflected in these portraits, surrounded the assembled college. At the end of the room, on a raised dais, was the high table. Here sat, facing the college, the faculty and president of the college.

No one was permitted to eat until grace was given by a classics scholar, who was required to recite an appropriate text in Latin—all by memory. Then the food was brought in on huge pure silver trays. The silverware was also pure silver. It was simplicity and elegance. All would go smoothly, unless the scholar made a mistake in the Latin verse, in which case, the wrath of the assembled would descend on the poor scholar. The wrath was pretend only, but it was loud and lively. This poor devil would be compelled to drink two quarts of beer in one fell swoop and stumble away in disgrace. If any member of the college should mention a lady's name, including the queen's name, or mention a swear word, a similar fate would await this poor fellow. This was called a sconce, and it had a powerful effect in keeping table conversation on a somewhat more lofty level.

One of the most pleasant and challenging assignments at the college was to be chairman of the dance committee. The college held a spring dance in late May, right after examinations, and it was a time to celebrate and take a fling before going "down" or leaving Oxford, for who knew where.

How this task was bestowed on me is still a mystery. Word just reached me via many friends who seemed to know everything about these matters, and before I could figure out how this happened, I was busy getting the job done. There were some giddy moments. One was to put fig leaves on the naked statuary and receive word from the president of the college, Mr. Hardie, that he disapproved of that desecration of the natural beauty of the artwork. We complied but did so slowly. We wanted to set the stage for something more provocative than the waltz.

The dance went very well until the wee hours in the morning. We ran out of whisky for the band and ran out of money to buy more, which was then available only from private sources.

But by then, nobody cared, and those who remained were in no condition to know what was going on. Dances in England are serious stuff.

The examinations at the end of my two-year stay would test every bit of me. They were administered by the university, not the college. It was one thing to carry on a particular free market point of view to one's tutor, but it was quite a different matter to do so in front of a university examiner. These took a very academic point of view. They were there, they believed, to ensure high standards of received dogma, whatever the field. In short, they were not interested in my point of view. They were interested in whether I knew their point of view.

I decided to give it a try anyway. The written examination was in a large room filled with people, and two of the proctors, who were also examiners, stood above my chair and read what I was writing as I was writing. So I knew from this special attention that this was going to be a different examination from the usual.

The examination consisted of two parts. The written and an oral defense of what had been written. For the oral, you were lined up in chairs outside an examination room. All of this was inside a separate building whose only purpose was to give examinations.

My name was called, and I was ushered into the actual examination room by two escorts. As I entered the room, my name was announced, and one of the three examiners invited me to sit down. Thank goodness. All of this protocol made me almost speechless. I guess it was intended to do this or at least intimidate me.

The room was large, without pictures or any decoration. There were no books nor were there bookcases. A large green felt cloth covered the table. It was a room meant for strictly business, and the business of these gentlemen was to grill me to see what I knew that they felt was important.

The first of these three examiners led off with basic questions about economic theory. I answered the way I knew he wanted and then said why this was deficient. He turned his head away, dismissing my remarks.

The next examiner was hard on his trail and took my thoughts as being bad judgment. He was pretty harsh. This went on for twenty minutes or so, but it seemed unending.

In addition to the economics questions, there were questions concerning British politics and modern British philosophy, all of which formed a broad field to cover.

Then the third examiner started to laugh, made some good-natured comments, and the first examiner decreed the meeting was finished. There must have been many private jokes that I never caught, judging from the looks between the examiners. All of this was very disconcerting.

I thanked everybody and walked out of the door, which was opened just at the right moment by the two escorts. How they ever knew when to do this remains a mystery to me to this day.

My examiners concluded that I should receive an Oxford

degree, and then, amazingly, determined that I should be given honors, but the lowest level.

Of course, I was surprised when I learned of the news—actually in the *Times* newspaper of London. I simply read that I had been awarded the degree with honors. It could easily have gone the other way. So it was, and so it remains. I was lucky beyond all expectation.

Chapter 10
The Federal Reserve Bank
1960 to 1963

My first real job—a job that begins a career—was at the Federal Reserve Bank of Cleveland.

This was the most difficult job of my career. I found myself over my head in political positions which I was required to accept. I also found myself in a less than friendly environment, which drained my strength, and I did not perform to my best ability.

Everything started out well and then went downhill.

I had applied for a summer job earlier, before I left for Oxford, and was cordially treated by the research department. Tuffy Cutler, an economist who was also the manager of the office, interviewed me and asked why I didn't start to work right then and there. He was ready to hire me, but only as a full-time employee. He said that the bank did not hire summer help.

So when I returned from England, I looked him up again. He remembered me and hired me on the spot. In those days, there were few economists, and if you had an advanced degree, you were a rare bird indeed.

I was hired as an associate economist. This was the lowest level of the professional staff. It was also the lowest title that gave you your own office with a door on it, which by custom you never closed. My salary was $7,240 per year. That was a princely sum at the time.

The research department was the fastest growing department at the bank. It consisted of about twenty people, including clerks. The remainder of the bank was engaged in examining banks for safety and processing checks.

The whole Federal Reserve System was gearing up to face the political scene of postwar economic programs where the economy would be driven by government programs and be directed overall by central planning. The Federal Reserve was at the center, because it literally created the money which made everything possible.

The research department of the Cleveland Federal Reserve Bank was important because it spread the word of all of these activities to the local scene in Ohio, parts of West Virginia, Kentucky, and western Pennsylvania. This was done through research reports on the economy, radio broadcasts, and public-speaking appearances before Rotary, Kiwanis, and other service organizations.

This presence was intended to be positive. And there were very definite things I could say and not say. For example, I could say that the interest rates under the Federal Reserve's tenure always followed rates in the market. I could not say that the

Federal Reserve set interest rates or that it controlled them. But of course, it did this. It was part of the broader plan to protect the immense power of this central bank from public criticism.

Yet to a young turk such as myself, fresh from heated discussions in graduate seminars, all of this appeared to be pussy-footing. I didn't fit comfortably into the colorless image that the bank had so carefully crafted.

Then there was the thorny issue of inflation. The bank claimed that inflation was caused by excess demand, whatever that might mean. Research on the subject by Milton Friedman at the University of Chicago had shown conclusively that inflation was caused by excess growth of money supply. Milton Friedman was denounced by certain members of the research staff. I was baffled by this. There wasn't any reason to take such a position, except a political reason.

Tuffy was my friend from the start. He had been through political storms earlier in his career and, I suspect, felt kindly toward me because I was probably like he had been years before. But I was upsetting to the decorum of the bank, and there were limits to his help.

Then Maury Mann came to the department as a new director of research. Maury did not like any independence and took a dislike to me. That made my performance go downhill. I had never worked under an adversarial environment before, and it was an eye-opening experience.

And so even my best talents, including writing, turned out to be below par. Whatever I did seemed to crash.

The office next to mine was that of Bob Brunner, who was given the tasks of revising whatever I wrote. Bob was a friend, and we shared many moments together. He invited me to his home, and his wife cooked many dinners for me. Still, it was an uneasy friendship.

The guards at the bank were always my friends. When I would walk through the door, they would smile and say hello. Others with me would remark that I was being given special recognition, and they wondered why. The answer was that all of the guards were master masons in one of the many Masonic lodges throughout Cleveland. I am also a master mason. And when a new person was elevated in the Masonic order, the bank guards showed up for the ceremony. I never mentioned this to anybody who wasn't a Mason. And I suspected that the Masonic order permeated the bank's officer ranks. It was the inner group; I had reason to believe, quietly making sure that all was well.

At this time, I had the special privilege of raising my father to a master mason in the Lakewood lodge. Usually fathers do this to their sons. We never did much with the lodge, but it was a happy and major moment in our mutual lives, as these things go.

Then at a particularly difficult moment for me, Noel McBride, an industrial economist at the bank, left to become the economist for the Cleveland Trust Bank. Rumor had it that he had been offered twelve thousand dollars a year, which nobody could quite believe. That left a gap in the research group, and so I was promoted to the rank of full economist and got a raise. I wondered how I could be doing such a poor job and then be elevated.

About the same time that this happened, I heard through the grapevine that the Agency for International Development had asked the bank for an economist to join a special task force in Bolivia. At first I had been selected, but second thoughts about my so-called poor performance caused my name to be withdrawn.

How lucky that was—that I never was a part of the AID mission. It turned out that this mission was a front for a CIA plan to eradicate communists in the mountains. Instead of removing the communists, it was they who removed the AID mission, which I later heard was mostly wiped out after many American lives were lost. So never again would I bemoan hardships at work that came my way. They may really be saving my life.

After a few years had elapsed, I began to make speeches throughout the region. I liked this work. It got me out of the office, and I really enjoyed meeting businessmen of all sorts and kinds. I liked the fact that most of them had many customers. They were upbeat people, and I felt closer to them than to the Federal Reserve. I would trade all of the prestige of the bank for their position.

One area of training on this job was writing. I had always been a good writer, but what I did at the bank was to hone in my skill. I learned the importance of revising, revising and revising. Each time the writing would get shorter, sharper and better. I have carried out that lesson through the years, and added to it as I went along.

Mostly these were small businessmen. I knew realistically that their life was not mine, but it started me thinking that there were other pastures beside the bank. About this time, Tuffy began to drop hints of what other former economists were doing. In one instance, the hint went right over my head. I missed it, but Maie, who was with me, caught it and mentioned it to me. There must have been other nudges and hints that I missed also.

I smoked cigarettes during this period. Everybody, or just about everybody, smoked. Rooms were hazy. There was a brown coating on mirrors. Cars were filled with the dense smoke of these little white tubes. I quit without difficulty. I knew that they were not good for health, despite advertising which quoted doctors as authorities that said there was no throat irritation from smoking. It was all rubbish.

I read at this time Alfred P. Sloan's recently published book, *My Years with General Motors*, and it had a profound effect on my thinking. He seemed to have the answers to running a business, and I wanted to be a part of this effort. His thinking was summarized best, I thought, in the work of corporate planning. Here, I thought, was the essential core to successful business.

And it so happened that a company in Cleveland, Ferro Corporation, was looking for somebody to do this work. I wanted that job more than anything else. So I applied for the position and was fortunate to have as a friend and fellow economist Jim Dawson, who was on the company's board.

At the same time, a position at Standard Oil of Ohio, in

something they called economic marketing, opened up, and I interviewed this company as well. I didn't realize the power of this position at the time. It could have led to a top-level spokesman for the oil industry. But at that time, nobody, including me, had any idea of the future importance of oil. The United States was drenched in oil. It was just another ordinary commodity, or so it seemed at the time.

Ferro took a long time to make up their mind. I suspect they had other candidates beside myself. And I later heard that they earlier had hired someone for the task who did not work out. I waited patiently.

Finally, word arrived that I was hired. I was in seventh heaven.

During early time with the Federal Reserve Bank, I was footloose and fancy-free. At this time, I met Dale Durkee at the bank, and he introduced me to his circle of friends who docked boats at the river harbor Vermillion, thirty-five miles west of Cleveland. These included Ralf Schubert, Dick Marshner, Ray Brehm, Bob Dodd, Beth, Gail, Jack, and Jane Burke. And there were others. We were a portable club.

Usually, the group met at a fish restaurant, McGarvy's, which was close to the mouth of the Vermillion River. Several people had sailboats—two had power boats, and the talk always included something about the boats and the weather. Lake Erie is notorious as a dangerous lake, because it is shallow and kicks up high waves with even a moderate breeze. All of this was summertime fun.

Sometimes we would get caught. One time, this involved me. I had bought a star sailboat, which is a twenty-three-foot racing sailboat. I was coming back from Put-in-Bay, which is one of the beautiful islands in Lake Erie, about thirty miles west of Vermillion. Harriet Drapeski was with me, and we got caught in a sudden storm. The small engine failed, and the wind was so strong that we were being pushed across the lake in ever-heavier seas. It was getting dark, and we were very scared. The boat couldn't take much more weather.

Then a light appeared in the distance. It came closer. So I flashed the boat with my flashlight, which did work, thank heavens. Nothing happened. Then Harriet said, "Give them an SOS signal." I did that, and the huge power boat—at least sixty feet—threw me a line and then towed my little sailboat to the closest harbor. I never felt so grateful as when I stood on solid land. The boat's captain said he saw my flashing, but it didn't mean anything to him until he saw the SOS. I am alive today; I am sure because of Harriet's head. I liked Harriet, but her father thought I was trouble and didn't want to see me around the house. So we went our separate ways. I wonder what happened to her.

In the winter, the group went skiing. This was tame stuff compared with today's Rocky Mountain or Sierra skiing. And skiing equipment was much more primitive. There were lots of tow ropes, few chair lifts, and no enclosed cabins. The skis were made of wood, and stylish clothes were three sweaters on top of one another. But we had fun and never dreamed of today's technical improvements, which can enable the ordinary person to ski very nicely right at the beginning. It's not like those days, when flops and falls were every minute.

As my days with the Federal Reserve Bank were drawing to a close, my grandfather's life was also coming to a close, and my life with my wife-to-be was just opening. All three very important events happened within a few days of one another. It makes me wonder if there is something more than chance in life.

My grandfather's passing was a relief to my father, who had taken care of him during almost a decade of gradual failure. His mind was gone, and he was a big man to move about. My father never complained, but faithfully, very faithfully, kept him clean and fed. The house was torn apart and didn't smell very good. My aunt Jean told me not to take Maie, my bride-to-be, to my grandfather's house. I wanted Maie to see everything, the good and the bad, so I took her and held my breath. Maie was already a doctor, and I felt that doctors can see everything. Maie didn't say much afterward, but I felt that I had done the right thing and shown her all.

Three days after my grandfather's funeral, Maie and I were married. Somebody asked me if I should postpone the wedding. I didn't want to do this. My grandfather would have wanted no delay in our wedding. He was that kind of man. And so we went ahead, flying to Winnipeg the day after he rested in his final place, along with my grandmother, and eventually my father and his second wife, Marge, at Crown Hill Cemetery in Twinsburg, Ohio.

Chapter 11

Maie

1960 to Present

Maie has been a gift to me from heaven. I cannot imagine my life without her. The thought of her being away leaves me distraught. There is no one nor anything that could fill her presence.

It seems that we have been together for time without end. Each day I say to myself, "Please, oh please, let us have more days to come." For nearly fifty years, this has been granted. How exquisite this has been.

I met Maie in an almost Hollywood manner.

I had gone to Puerto Rico in February, 1963, for a vacation. The winters in Cleveland are harshest that month, because we always had a teaser warm day or thaw that month, and then we got hit with the coldest weather for the year. It always happened, and I wanted to be someplace else.

I couldn't decide whether to visit my mother, who was then

living in Los Angeles, or go to someplace in the islands, like Puerto Rico.

I was in New York for something, and I went out to La Guardia airport and saw an Eastern Airlines poster which advertised San Juan, Puerto Rico, for ninety-nine dollars. That was exactly the same price as a flight to Los Angeles.

I walked up to the ticket counter and told the young lady my dilemma, briefly, and asked her opinion. She looked befuddled and said something like, "They're both nice places." But the ticket agent next to her had been listening and shouted out, "Go to Puerto Rico. I just got back." I put my ninety-nine dollars down and boarded the Lockheed propeller plane and got comfortable for a long overnight flight.

The next day, I went to the beach and got sunburned.

Thus, on the second day I needed to stay inside and decided to do something cultural, like walk through the old fortress, El Morro, I think it was called. In one of the northernmost rooms was a model of the fortress as it was three hundred years ago.

I love maps and models and was glued to it for a long time, maybe half of an hour. Then two young girls were walking near the model. They paid no attention to it. I could see that they were cute. They started to walk away. I couldn't let this happen. What to do. I turned to them and asked what turned out to be the fateful question, "Which way is north?" I knew perfectly well which way was north. But that wasn't the point.

They turned to me, looked at each other, giggled, and said that they didn't have any idea. Well, that started the conversation.

We walked out of the fortress together and stopped at a sidewalk cafe, and I treated them to something to drink—nothing substantial; it was Coca Cola or some such bubbly drink.

We decided to have dinner together. That was nice. Then we talked about renting a car, and we talked about places to go. It was a wonderful idea, we all thought. We would split the cost three ways, making it really very cheap. The lowest priced rental was a Volkswagen bug, which I rented. We took a number of trips and got our money's worth from that rental. We went to several beaches away from the tourist zone; one was El Yunque, which had sand like white powder. We went to the mountains and to the rain forest.

We were coming back from a trip the night before I was to leave. Maie's accompanying friend, Tina, wanted to go to a sorority meeting of Zonta, I believe it was called. Apparently on that particular evening, members of this sorority met for inspiration and dinner all over the world. I had never heard of the organization. But I was delighted because it would give me a chance to be alone with Maie. Wouldn't you know, Tina got us lost on the way back; Zonta was finished, and my hopes were dashed.

We said goodbye at the airport. I gave Tina a necklace and Maie a toy dog with a windup tail that played "How Much Is That Doggie in the Window." I later learned that these gifts were a mystery to the two girls. They couldn't figure out which gift meant the most. There was no question in my mind. The doggie came first.

It was clear to me that something should happen. But after I returned to Cleveland, I was swamped with things to do. I kept Maie in mind but did nothing. And three weeks later, I had agreed to meet a fellow classmate from Oxford, Keith Kirkman, who rowed with me, for a skiing weekend in Canada.

Then came Maie's postcard from New York. Basically, it was an invitation to come to see her. That's all it took. I said to myself, "Let's go." I had no idea where Winnipeg was located, but that didn't matter. I wrote her back that I would be there in three weeks. I wrote Keith Kirkman also, and he wrote me back that he was not happy that I wouldn't be skiing. To this day, I have felt uncomfortable whenever I think of this. But Keith had to take second fiddle in this situation.

I arrived in Winnipeg and was royally treated by Maie's mother and father. Maie treated me better than royalty, and we had a smashing good time.

There were more trips to Winnipeg. On one trip, we were told to disembark the plane so that it could refuel. This was at Thunder Bay, where there were two planes a day leaving this outpost. I didn't hear the announcement to reboard. The plane started up, and I ran on to the field with my arms waving. They let me on.

On another occasion, I was seated next to someone who was traveling to visit his parents and also Maie. We just happened to be assigned these particular seats. In the course of the flight, we began to talk. I didn't have a clue as to what was going on, but thinking back, I am sure that Maie's friend, Len, caught on quickly. I was in the dark for the entire trip.

When we got off the plane, Len greeted his parents and left the airport. I looked around and couldn't find Maie. Finally, she emerged from behind a pillar. I was glad to see her. Only then did I realize that she was avoiding Len so that she could greet me alone.

That wasn't the end to Len. I asked Maie where she would like to have dinner that Saturday evening. She mentioned a fancy French place, where waiters wore gloves. I was very pleased with the restaurant, and we ordered chateaubriand for two. The next day, I left to return to Cleveland, and Len took Maie to the same restaurant, and he ordered the same chateaubriand. The waiter must have had quite a chuckle and wondered to himself who this young lady must be.

Maie's parents were hard workers. I recognized this right off the bat. After two visits, I felt uncomfortable just arriving and enjoying myself. So I asked her father what he needed to have done around the house. He was a bit surprised at the request but didn't miss a beat and said that the garage door was in need of some painting skills. We found a brush and some white paint, and while Maie took a rest that Saturday afternoon, I painted the door. I must have endeared myself to her father ever after by asking and doing this. I think that sold me to her parents. And what wonderful, loving, down-to-earth, and generous parents they were.

Maie was in Winnipeg. I was in Cleveland. It's difficult to carry on a romance with people a thousand miles apart. That was the logistics problem. We couldn't be flying back and forth each week. And we weren't ready yet to get married. We had met in February, and it was May, and something had to give way if we were to get to know each other better.

Maie had finished her medical studies at the University of Manitoba and had plans to study neuropathology, which is a medical specialty, in Toronto. That was closer, but still it was an eight-hour drive from Cleveland—still too far. The idea came to me—I don't think it was mine—but the idea came to us that she might continue her specialty studies in Cleveland, if there would be room for her and somebody would accept her as a student.

It so happened that Maie's close friend and medical school classmate, Garth Bray, had already made arrangements to continue his studies in neurology in Cleveland. Could Garth be of any help? Well, he was. He knew that the wife of his professor was a neuropathologist, and was interested in sponsoring a student. What good luck that was! After contacting this professor, Dr. Betty Banker, all was set for Maie to continue in Cleveland. All was set except Maie didn't have a visa to enter the United States as a student. These things involve lots of paper work and long waits.

That couldn't happen. It could take a year to get a visa. The reason was that the immigration law of the time allowed only one hundred people from Estonia, the country of Maie's birth, to immigrate each year to the United States, and that quota was backed up for several years into the future. Complicating matters, Maie, her brother, and parents were refugees from the Second Great War.

So I got on the phone and contacted my congressman and senators, as well as the ranking people on any congressional committee that had anything to do with immigration. I took a week to speak with everybody who was involved and wrote letters to back up my phone calls. Then I started phoning again. By this time, I knew whom to call. It turned out that there are special assistants to each congressman who handle these matters. Once you reach them, you're on your way, or that is how it was then.

Meanwhile, Maie was stuck in Winnipeg. But all of this commotion bore fruit. By early July, six weeks after we started this campaign, Maie heard from a United States envoy that she should pick up her visa, that it was ready for her to use.

Maie went to the right place the day she received notice. The representative of the United States government gave her the visa and said something that Maie has remembered ever after. He said that Maie must know somebody important in the government because he had never seen anybody get a visa of this type so quickly. Naturally, Maie was delighted and felt a bit like a privileged person.

Well, she was. But in fact, I was nobody special. What I did was work hard to get what I wanted. Persistence always counts for a lot. It was that simple and that important.

The sequel to this story is interesting. Six months after all of this happened, the professor with whom Maie had originally expected to study suddenly died. If Maie had gone to Toronto, she would have been left high and dry. There was no backup professor. Maie would not have been able to continue studying what interested her. The change and our plans to get married saved her career. Life is full of surprises like that.

So we were finally together. Actually, it took a lot of courage for Maie to come to Cleveland. I had not asked her to marry me. I had said we should be close to each other and see how things went. This was not a tremendously romantic way of doing things. As things were at the time, there was no doubt in my mind that we would get married. So there was nothing misleading. In fact, the whole situation was as careful as could be imagined. I suppose I should have been more dramatic or something. I am deeply thankful that Maie had enough confidence in me to keep going.

As it turned out, our going together amounted to just eight months, which is not a long time for these things. Especially in those days, when people went together for years and nobody thought anything unusual about it.

All of this put extra pressure on the engagement ring, as a symbol of our intentions, or rather my intention, because it was up to me to get one.

And in this department not everything went smoothly. But when you're looking forward to getting married, even a small hitch ruffles the feathers more than you would like. Maie's engagement ring was a big time event for her back in Cleveland in those days. We had talked about the ring, and I said we should go to Cowell and Hubbard, a jeweler on Euclid Avenue in downtown Cleveland.

They were open on Thursdays, which happened to be the day we were on my aunt Jean's front porch. Maie thought we were going to go to select the ring that day. I thought that was a good idea, but we started talking and laughing, and the time flew by. Soon, it was too late to go downtown. I later learned that Maie was terribly disappointed.

We did go to the jeweler the following Saturday and found just the ring she liked. But those hours from the front porch to the jeweler must have been very, very long for Maie.

I didn't have much extra cash, so the diamond was not large and, in fact, had a small flaw inside the stone. Maie was always uncomfortable with this flaw, so as a surprise gift on our twenty-fifth anniversary, I presented her with a new engagement ring with a perfect stone. Some things take time but are not forgotten.

Our wedding was just right. It was in a small Lutheran church in Winnipeg, with the ceremony performed by a young and slightly nervous pastor. During the ceremony, Maie's niece, Karin, who was about four years old, kept counting pennies from her little purse. Well, the purse was so small that she couldn't get the pennies back into the purse. So the pennies started to fall on the floor. Plink, plank, plunk! I started to hear these dropping sounds over the pastor's words. What in the world could that be? I wondered. Why doesn't somebody do something? Of course, it didn't matter or make any difference. But on important events, you want everything to be perfect. But it never is, and that's all right.

I wondered how much I should pay the pastor and asked several people. The consensus was fifteen dollars, which is the amount I gave him. I feel that I should have given him more. If I could find him now, I would gladly augment that sum. But I suppose that was the right amount for the time. Times were different, costs were different, and spending was different.

Our wedding was a blast. My aunt Jean got tanked and brought the house down. My cousin June was the life of the party. Maie and I didn't make fools of ourselves—maybe we should have. We just enjoyed it all. What a happy time it was.

Then came the honeymoon. When we finished the wedding, I knew I would be broke. There are big things and so many little things, and they all add up. So I went to see a lending officer at National City Bank for a seven-hundred-dollar loan. We planned to go to Mexico for a week, and I figured that amount would cover us. I had borrowed two thousand four hundred dollars a year earlier to buy a Corvair Chevy convertible and felt my good payment record would help with this new loan. This was an unsecured loan and was considered at the time to be a bit risky for a bank to make.

I got the loan, but not before some words at the loan committee. My friend John Albright, who worked for the bank, happened to hear about this loan. It was chosen by a senior officer of the bank to be an example of what he saw to be the deterioration of society—that a young couple did not save up for their wedding and honeymoon but went into debt for these events, particularly for the pleasure of a honeymoon. My name was well-known around that bank before he was through with me. I, of course, knew nothing of this. It was probably best that I didn't know. I repaid the loan ahead of time, in fact, and received an atlas of America from the bank for doing so.

We spent two days in Mexico City and five days at Acapulco. The time in Mexico City was uneventful. Mexico City is a big place, and we seemed not to find the beautiful or interesting parts. We did see two remarkable murals on outdoor walls and were surprised to see department stores that were similar to those in Cleveland.

We also were bumped from the rear, as we navigated our rental car through the streets. The driver motioned for us to pull over to the side of the road, which we did. He then proceeded to drive away into the traffic. The bump wasn't bad, and so we drove away as well. When we took the car back to the rental agent, he wasn't concerned either. It was all very strange. In the United States, there would have been a fuss and lots of paper work to fill out.

Acapulco was a resort with fancy buildings lining the beach. The best place was Las Brisas. We saved up to spend our last day and night there and enjoyed every minute of it.

The memorable event came on our trip back to Mexico City, which Maie won't let me forget. We were going along nicely, and Maie asked me what the red light on the dashboard meant. I looked and saw immediately that we were nearly out of gasoline. This was as we were deeply in the jungle, miles from nowhere.

What to do. What could you do but go on and see what

comes. We were seven miles from the mountain rim that surrounds Mexico City. We cut our speed to thirty miles per hour to save gas. And I stopped twice at houses to ask if they had any gas. The people I spoke with didn't speak Spanish but spoke only the native language of the Indian population. It was a terrible moment. I felt so helpless.

We kept going and finally reached the top of this rim. Then we started down. I turned off the motor, and we coasted five miles to the bottom where sure enough, there was a gasoline station. What a sigh of relief! A shortage of gasoline that would have taken us just ten feet less would have meant disaster.

In a very direct way, the surprises and unexpected turns of our honeymoon set the stage for nearly five decades of married life. We could not have imagined all the things that have happened to us in those years.

Most of all, it was Maie's good judgment and calm appraisal of the situation that kept us in good shape. In sickness and health, for better or worse, she was there.

Nothing illustrates this more than saving a life. She saved the life of every member of our family. In the case of my father, she noticed that he was walking strangely during one of his visits. So she invited one of her doctor friends to dinner, in order to observe him more carefully. They concluded that my father did indeed have a walking problem, but it was more serious than anyone had imagined. If he did not have brain surgery, he would soon be bedridden. Maie told him exactly whom to see in Cleveland when he returned home. My father took the advice, had the operation, and lived many years beyond. Her eagle eye and knowledge saved him.

She saved the life of her mother, Ema, as she was called by Maie. She was diagnosed with cancer in Canada, but instead of operating promptly to remove the growth, the doctors there postponed this treatment and did not propose to do anything for a number of months. Maie saw this as a terrible decision and, through her contacts with the medical establishment in Winnipeg and Canada, was able to schedule an operation promptly. That action enabled the surgeon to catch the growth before it had spread. She lived many more years as a consequence. Later on, Maie's mother passed away due to a different cause.

When Maie's father developed sudden intestinal problems that were life threatening and had turned down surgery, she flew from Palo Alto to his bedside in a Winnipeg hospital. He was distraught and was giving up his will to live. Maie spoke with him, with care and kindness, and brought him around to see that he could live for many years with happiness if he went on the surgeon's table. She talked about his grandchildren and how much they loved and needed him and that he was needed here now. He saw the light of Maie's persuasion, had the operation, and enjoyed many years of a good life. Maie understood instinctively what compassionate doctors always do for their patients.

We had frequent visits from Maie's brother, Enn. His first wife, May, died when she was still young; and Enn married again, to Millie. May was a lovely and gracious lady and was much missed. Millie is vivacious and matched Enn perfectly. Enn developed lung cancer when he was in his early seventies and died a few years later. He had a bright mind and, being an engineer by training, could fix just about anything.

May and Enn's two daughters have families that we are with frequently. His daughter Karin married Scott Chisholm, and they have a daughter, Lisa, and a son, Andrew. Scott is a master chef, and whenever he visits us, he takes over the kitchen to the rejoicing of Maie. Scott is one of the brightest members of our family, and he works on patents. Lisa and Andrew are contestants in the Canadian triathlon competition, and both are highly ranked. Their endurance is phenomenal and much admired.

Daughter Kirsten married Lyle McLeod. They also have a daughter and son. Alison is an artist and is her own person. Callum is a fun-loving young man, who has had a lifelong passion for animals. I predict that he will reach a high level in his chosen profession. He bears all of the early earmarks of this.

All of this family lives in Canada. Another relative we see is Maie's cousin, Helmi Karlson, who also lives in Canada. Helmi and her companion, Rita, give me bouts of laughter. I mean this in the most positive way. I see the humor of Helmi while it escapes most of the family. I'm glad that I can enjoy it.

Maie loves to cook. She is happiest when a special new dish comes out just right. Most of her choices are in the nature of Italian cuisine, but she loves to make her favorites of Estonian menus, as well as German and some French. You can often see her working on a dinner, taking several hours to prepare special sauces, and locating unusual ingredients at one of the food stores in the area. And such delicious fragrances that waft from the kitchen.

She always seems to be making cookies. Christmas is cookie time, with half a dozen or more specialties being prepared at one time. It's my favorite time to cruise the kitchen and sample what is just then out of the oven.

I suppose cookie time is a most happy time for Maie. What a way to be busy.

During the Christmas season, when our children were young, Maie would prepare an Estonian feast for our friends and neighbors. She would cover the dining room table with the delights of this northern country's favorite delectables. The house would be full of young parents and children. What a task this would be for Maie. Yet she loved every minute of those times.

When we were first married and watching every penny with great care, Maie's mother would weave a material on her loom and then cut and fit dresses and clothing for Maie as well as some beautiful garments for me. I continue to wear the plaid robe that she made for me forty years ago. Maie has kept many of these dresses and other things, and they are arrayed in the basement on hangers. They appear as a silent reminder of her tour through the years. Each one is unique and beautiful. They all fit perfectly or did at one time.

Maie is never demanding of luxury goods or even standard things. She has a saving nature for most instances.

The story of how we got her first car tells this to perfection. We had just moved to Brecksville. Maie worked downtown in Cleveland as I did also. I would swing by Metropolitan General Hospital where Maie worked in the evening and in the morning would drop her off in a similar fashion. But Maie needed her own car. One car was not enough out in the near countryside. Moreover, my car was a small pocket-sized car, a Corvair convertible that couldn't carry very much.

So the time came quickly for us to find another car—for a small amount of money. I looked in the newspapers for several weeks and saw a 1958 Oldsmobile model eighty-eight, and this was the super deluxe model. I went over to look at it, and it looked in good shape—remembering that in Cleveland, a six-year-old car has already suffered six winters of salt and snow.

I decided to buy the car and paid three hundred twenty-five dollars. I called Maie to tell her the news, which I thought was good news. Driving to pick up Maie so we could bring the new car home, a sudden pang of remorse set in. What if Maie didn't like this car? It had more chrome on it than any car that has ever been made, before or after. There were streaks of chrome everywhere. I told Maie that the car had lots of chrome, but I was not sure she would want to drive it and be seen alighting from it.

What a good sport she was. She had no problems with the looks of the car, got into the car, and drove it home. Much later, she told me that she was in fact embarrassed to be seen in this bright green ugly car, with lots of shiny metal plastered all over the sides, front, and rear. But it was a good and reliable car. And Maie never once complained about its looks.

Nor did Maie flinch an eye when it went away. It turned out that the ladies of a high-class organization—Planned Parenthood—were among the first to receive donations of cars. I served as a director of the Cleveland chapter for several years. One lady wanted to launch the program properly and gave away a vintage Rolls Royce. The *Cleveland Plain Dealer*, which was the local morning newspaper, ran a feature article on the program, showed Maie's Oldsmobile in a picture with three of the senior ladies polishing this old car. The headline read, "Car Donations from an Olds to a Rolls."

Maie was mentioned in the article. I thought she would feel somewhat embarrassed, because anyone who knew that car would have laughed at the pretentious overtones the article gave it. Maie didn't miss a beat and never let this bother her. What a relief for me.

Maie always looks after me, to be sure that I look just right when I go out of the house. In fact, she won't let me out unless I pass her inspection. It is a bit of a bother to be brushed up this way, but it is always reassuring and comforting to know you are being looked after so well.

A number of years ago, she got a worrisome reading from her mammogram and had a breast removed. With this, you're always living with a possible time bomb. But we don't dwell on the issue. Maie lives for the present, and there have been many wonderful years since the event came up, and we count ourselves as part of the lucky ones.

Maie never cared for my star-class sailing boat. She would go out in the boat, but never with any enthusiasm. I felt that I was pushing the boat to get anything from it.

That was all right. When you get married, something always has to go. So I sold the boat. It was fun while it lasted.

The story of one of Maie's relatives from Estonia is inspiring, and I am pleased that I could be a part of it. Her cousin's son, Andres Reial, was a young man when his grandfather in Canada, Uncle Eini, passed away, leaving a good sum of money to his three children in Estonia, but with the proviso that none of the money would be confiscated by the communists in Estonia.

The decision was made to buy him a computer in this country and ship it to Andres as his personal inheritance. So far, so good. I came into the picture as the person who would buy the computer, secure export permission to send it, and make sure he received it. Just about everything that could go wrong went wrong. The United States export controls suddenly were made more stringent the month I went to buy the computer, as a way of tightening the rope around the neck of the communists. But I did secure the most powerful computer allowed under the law, bought it and shipped it.

The very same week it was shipped, there was an earthquake in the south of Armenia, and delivery of all nonofficial shipments was interrupted. So six months later, I received a phone call from a U.S. Treasury agent concerning the computer which had been sidetracked to a warehouse in New Jersey. The agent wanted to know why I was shipping what was now considered to be equipment to help an enemy of the United States. I explained everything and convinced him I was shipping the computer to help a young man in his studies. That worked; I paid the storage fee, and the computer went on its way.

What a terrific gift this was! Andres was the only person in Estonia who had a personal computer. He did distinguished work, was noticed by a college group, got a scholarship to study in the United States, and graduated from the University of Virginia with a doctorate in computer science, and we were delighted to see him receive his diploma. He is now on his way, having married a Peruvian girl—at whose wedding we attended—working in Sweden. How wonderful it is to have crossed paths to help such deserving people.

Maie is really an unrecognized artist. Occasionally, she will draw a picture of something, and it is quite remarkable. She once drew a picture of our second dog, Woody, and it was beautiful. She also sketched our first dog, Patches, which hangs on my office wall.

Perhaps the closest she has come to serious artistic work is china painting. This is where a vase or plate or a cup is decorated with a painting. Often, the painting is flowers, particularly roses. The paint pigment is finely ground glass. This is then put into a kiln and baked at one thousand five hundred degrees Fahrenheit for several hours, and the glass is fused to the china.

Maie never competed in glass-based decorations, but if she had, she would surely have won a prize.

I wish that she would pursue her artistic talent. Yet it is also reassuring to have an undeveloped talent of any type. There would be plenty to do, whatever might come.

Among the people who have visited us in California and we have visited in their homes, those who live in Estonia are probably the most remarkable. These people live eight thousand miles away. They are the relatives who were left in Estonia when the Russians invaded and who suffered under their tyranny. Some, not with us today, lost their lives.

Maie and I first visited these relatives nearly thirty years ago, and the bridge to these remarkable people is now a short one. Male Kuut is a steady standby who looks after us whenever we are in Estonia. Anna Noori shows a grace and gentleness that belies her brutal years in Siberia. She magnificently transcends those years and now grows delicious fruits and vegetables.

Andrus and Anu Ansip have become essential people in Estonia. She is prominent in the medical life of Estonia, and he is prime minister. We have enjoyed trips to the inner parts of Estonia in their company, as we slip by untouched forests and freshwater lakes. Andrus has guided his country in a way which has maintained its independence and kept the country united. As I look ahead, he will almost certainly be called upon in ways that we now can't imagine, and he will prevail.

Perhaps the most upsetting thing in Maie's life is our basement, which is full of discarded everything. Maie does not like to throw away anything. She says that the years she lived with a lack of virtually everything when she was growing up have made her reluctant to discard things that could still be useful in some unknown, future way. Her father was the same way.

As a result, in order to keep the basement from bursting at the seams, Maie has resorted to packing things more tightly in more and more boxes. Now when you go down to the basement there are piles of boxes over your head. She manages to keep a good remembrance of where things are packed. This is nothing less than amazing, since some boxes are nearly fifty years old.

I have tried to show people this incredible place, but Maie won't let anybody set foot into the basement. The whole situation is good for lots of laughter from my point of view, but Maie takes it all very seriously.

And I suppose laughter has been a major reason we have been able to withstand the rough waters that invariably come our way. Often, there are no other answers. You just have to accept what fate brings you, and as hard as it is, you have to look upon it with a certain amount of detachment and not let it get you down. Laughter helps, even when the issue is tragic. As sad and terrible as Alan's loss, it helps to remember the funny moments and laugh again at something he did when he was little.

Maie is the principal reason we have been able to accumulate some assets in our lifetime. I had nothing when we got married, and Maie didn't have anything that amounted to much either.

Her willingness to save and go without and reuse and to be careful enabled us to put away something all of the time. It was never very much, but it established the habit of saving. This habit was more valuable than the amount of money that was involved during the early years of our being together. That set the stage for handling larger sums later. I have observed that it is the wife who sets the stage for savings or a lack of savings, not the husband. He invariably wants his wife to be happy. If she wants to spend their last cent, or even more, if she allows debt to accumulate, then that will be the financial pattern for that family. And it is savings which is the foundation of the financial plan for that family. The only families that have accumulated assets, I have observed, are those with a positive savings pattern. The higher the savings, the higher the asset accumulation. It is really that simple—and that is difficult for many people. But it works.

Maie always wanted our family to be warmly dressed when we went outdoors. She made sure that Alan and Sylvi, especially, were bundled up, ready for any cold blasts that might come. There is something more than warmth in this. It is the feeling of personal concern as you step out of the door. You know that at least your first step on your journey has the love of someone who cares. That is Maie.

Chapter 12

Brecksville

1965 to 1970

After saying goodbye to the Federal Reserve as an economist, I walked into the Ferro Corporation offices as manager of corporate planning.

The immediate difference between the two jobs was that I was earning eleven thousand six hundred dollars per year at my new task, much above what the bank paid me. That meant Maie and I could buy a nice house. This was a big deal for us.

We had been living in the world's smallest apartment on Valley Road in Cleveland's near-west side, paying $92.50 each month. There was a bedroom that fitted a double bed and nothing else. The living room accommodated a couch and a chair. We had a party in this place, and half of our guests were in the hall.

We started looking for a house right away. We thought we wanted to build the perfect house, and we found a lot on Calvin Drive in Brecksville, Ohio, that fitted that bill perfectly.

We chose Brecksville as the community we wanted to live in because it was mostly rural and was easy to get to work from any street in metropolitan Cleveland. At this time, Maie was working at the Metropolitan General Hospital, and Ferro was not far from Brecksville as well.

We bought a lot with a magnificent catalpa tree and hired an architect. We poured over plans with great excitement. Then we put the plans out to bid by contractors and received a big shock. We had planned to spend up to thirty thousand dollars in total, and the bids were well over forty thousand dollars.

We remembered a house we had looked at sometime before, which was located on Station Road. We looked again, and within a week bought the place for twenty-seven thousand five hundred dollars. Later, we sold the lot on Calvin Drive for what we paid for it.

The house had three bedrooms, a bath and a half, a lovely living room, kitchen, and a large screened-in porch. The rooms were really quite small, but we didn't realize this because anything would have seemed spacious after our postage-stamp apartment on Valley Road.

The setting of this house was beyond belief. It was perched on the top of a hill in what had one time been an apple orchard, with two and one-quarter acres of land. It looked down into a park and a river valley as that river fed into the Cuyahoga River, which was the main river of Cleveland.

You could see storms roll in, as if you were in the clouds. Then in springtime, there were literally hundreds of daffodils, as the previous owners, Fred and Gracil Peck, had carefully planted them in artistic clumps.

The house was heated by tunnels of hot air which were under the floor that you would stand on. So in the winter, the floors were always warm and the house seemed to simply radiate heat—which it did in a comfortable and inefficient manner. That didn't matter. Heat was cheap in those days, and the comfort of that house was a luxury I have not enjoyed anywhere else.

We visited all of the local churches, and all were like churches we had known elsewhere. We did join the Congregational Church and have been members of this church afterward because we felt close to a number of people who attended, including Betty and Roger Gifford, who were our next-door neighbors.

Our first years in that house, my first years with a wonderful company, Ferro, and our first child, Sylvi—we had truly found—or perhaps the word should be "we had truly put together our bliss on earth." We would never be more happy. My father lived nearby; my mother visited us frequently from Florida. Maie's folks loved to visit us from icy Winnipeg, Manitoba. All was well, safe, and nothing was threatening. How would anybody want to change anything?

My dad was never one to whoop up the humor in a situation or to be the first to see the lighter side of an event. He always wanted to keep his cool and appear responsible, whatever that might mean.

This got carried to an extreme one time he came over to

visit. It was a usual visit, and Maie had done her best with the meal, which was better than in any restaurant. Well, my dad kept wanting to tell us something, and I, being clueless to it all, simply talked on. After they left, Maie said that my father had something to tell us, and Marge, his second wife, was strangely silent. Maie guessed that they were going to have a baby.

I got on the phone—they had barely left an hour earlier—and asked my dad if he had wanted to tell us something. He said why yes, he had indeed wanted us to know—that he and Marge were going to have a baby in a few months. We were completely overjoyed. Maie started to count the age of Marge, and I told her not to do this, that it was already too late to think of that.

The baby, Guilford, arrived in a few months and was a great joy to my dad and Marge, who was my dad's second wife, They truly doted on him. Then two months later, Sylvi arrived. I'm not sure there was great affection between them when they were little. But as time has passed, I feel that their mutual regard has grown, and they realize how fortunate we feel ourselves to be in having both.

At this time, June Gill, my cousin who lived in New Castle, Pennsylvania, died suddenly. I had played with her as a child. She was three years older than I. She always loved to have fun. When I was in high school, she would come to visit at Christmas time, and we would go on a shopping tour which was really a tour of upscale watering holes. And what fun we would have. When we were younger, she always brought new games to play when she visited.

Her death was from an abortion. That made it all so tragic, because it need not have been. I had a dream the night she died. In this dream, I was being swept round and round, and I became dizzy. I never explored this dream and the possible connection to her last moments, and to this day, I really don't want to go any further.

There was one thing that came down the pike that would have changed everything. I was thirty-six years old at this time, and the Vietnam war was heating up. President Johnson needed more men to go to that jungle. It was a very unpopular war, and many potential army men were escaping the military draft by fleeing to Canada. That left fewer young men to be called up in the eighteen- to twenty-six-year-old group. News reports said that there were virtually no men left in that category for the armed service.

I was thirty-six years old when I received a notice to report for a physical examination. This was a preliminary step to the process of being drafted. The next step, if I passed the physical examination, would be an interview by the local draft board, which was number 30. This was the same board that my grandfather had been chairman years earlier. Then if they said yes, there would be an induction notice. Then basic training. Then Vietnam. I passed the physical.

The interview was all that separated me from a uniform. I arrived at the appointed hour and was invited to sit down, which I did. Now during the previous four years, I had been teaching economics at Cleveland State University. In fact, I had become a popular instructor both with students as well as my fellow faculty members. I had done this because the call had gone out that this new university needed qualified people to teach many different disciplines. But economics was in most demand, and there were virtually no economists in Cleveland at that time. I also liked earning extra money to help out at the end of the month.

There were three men on the draft board. One was a labor union official. I recall he was a shop steward. One was a small businessman, and the third was a retiree. Right after I sat down, they zeroed in on my teaching. They wanted to know all about it. Then the labor leader started to rant and rave about students who he believed were in college only to avoid the draft. I listened and sweated. What in the world could I say? He might be putting me in the same category, and the conclusion to that was, well, obvious.

I waited for him to get his feelings out in the air. Then came the moment for me to respond. I crossed my fingers. I said that many people thought this way, but my experience in teaching was that the students in classes were truly interested in learning and making their mark on the world and that they were sincere and dedicated to that end. I said that the draft was not a motivating factor, as I found things. He quieted down, and I was excused.

One week later, I received the dreaded letter from the draft board. I could barely open it. The letter said I had been reclassified to category 2A. That meant I was deferred due to an essential occupation. I like to feel that standing up for my students made the difference.

On top of all of this, my job at Ferro was going well. In fact, it was going better than I had ever expected. The work started out slowly and then kept on improving.

When I arrived on my first day of work, I was greeted by my boss, who insisted that I call him by his first name, George. He was executive vice president and reported to the president, Harry Marks. My title was manager of corporate planning.

First of all, George had no place to put me. After he greeted me, he asked me to be seated and walked around the offices to see if there might be space somewhere for me. There wasn't. But finally somebody found a closet which was presented to me as a temporary spot. I was not disturbed by this. My head was in the clouds. This was just exactly the job I wanted. Where I worked wasn't that important to me, and prestigious offices didn't mean a thing.

But George had a more basic problem with corporate planning. He didn't know what it was, and he didn't know what I should be doing. It didn't help, I later found out, that somebody else had held the job previously and had struck out.

George and I quickly became good business friends. For some reason, he respected me. Perhaps it was simply the way I handled myself. He liked a touch of restraint, somebody who was good with numbers and was open to suggestions. I had some ideas about planning that were based on Alfred Sloan's book, but I had no experience or authority on the subject. And I didn't want to be too pushy at the start.

We decided that I should attend a week's training in the subject by the American Management Association in New York City. This was a good idea. It gave me something to start from.

I boiled down all of the talk and literature to a simple four-part program, which we would prepare for each of the seven divisions of the company. I would work with the general manager of each of these divisions, and jointly we would submit this work to the managing committee and senior management for their review. Basically, through this work, the division manager would show where he was expected to be five years from now and what he would need to get there.

It was all very simple. And it was logical. But I still got disagreement along the way—nothing serious, but the politics of any organization have to be reckoned with. George watched this aspect of my work carefully. He knew that politics could ruin anything. But I negotiated those shoals pretty well.

Only once did he intervene. It involved the vice president and director of research, Ralph Bevis. This man was driving me crazy. He wanted to change everything. I went along at first with the work that involved his division. But then he wanted to change what he had already changed. Then he blocked anything from happening. That impasse led to my reporting to Harry Marks, the president, who told Ralph Bevis to mind his business and told me to get the job done.

Harry Marks and I got along famously, and he showered opportunities on me. The most important was to make me secretary of the managing committee. This meant I would attend all of the meetings of the committee that governed the company. I was, in effect, their equal. I was the only one who visited all the nooks and crannies of the company, and I became the best informed person as to what was going on—really going on.

Harry treated me as a special person everywhere. It almost amounted to smothering. At the company picnics, he spent all of his time with Maie and me. I felt I was at work. It was almost too much. But how could I complain?

Despite all of this deference, I felt I was stuck in a staff position. I yearned to run my own division or at least my own business.

And so when Sam Wolpert of Predicasts, Inc. came along, I was ripe for picking. Predicasts was a new economics and marketing company that sold forecasts of almost everything. The company had grown rapidly for almost ten years. Sam offered me the position of director of research.

Everyone advised me not to take the job, that it was fraught with problems. I was headstrong and accepted the position.

The company went into a tailspin the day I arrived, and I left the company three months after I started.

How could I have done such a thing? Ferro asked me to return. I was so crushed and embarrassed that I couldn't accept.

There I was—going from on top of the world to unemployed. If I had simply stayed with Ferro, my future would have been assured.

I began to look for work. That wasn't easy, since the country was in the midst of a serious recession, and staff positions were first to be cut back, much less hired.

But I had done something while I was at Ferro that would prove to be valuable at this time. I had written pieces for a small business publication called the *Commercial and Financial Chronicle*. I had, thus, a published record. This is what virtually nobody else in staff positions had done. And I was fortunate that the predictions in these articles had turned out to be correct.

I had also written an article titled "Can 1929 Happen Again?" which was published in the magazine *Business Horizons*. This publication came from the University of Indiana. In fact, the economics department invited Maie and me to visit the university during a weekend that included the opera *Carmen* being performed in the sports stadium.

CBS Nationwide News must have been short on news one day, and so they ran a five-minute review of the article on the air and mentioned my name several times. Of course, this knocked the socks off Harry Marks as he listened to it in his car while driving home.

The article and broadcast put me in a special group of business advisors who had one foot in business and another in the halls of scholarship. Corporations liked that for their corporate staff.

So I sent out one thousand four hundred résumés with a copy of the article, and six weeks later, I had received four job offers, One was to join a new institutional brokerage firm in Cleveland called Raulston & Co., the farm equipment producer Massey Fergusson, the plumbing manufacturer American Standard, and Stanford Research Institute. Everybody said to go to Stanford, which I did.

There was also a special reason that I chose Stanford Research Institute, and that involved Maie. She had been having recurring bouts of bronchial infections, which were probably caused by soot in the Cleveland air and a weakened condition from the deprivations and infections of a displaced-persons camp after the Second World War. The air in Palo Alto, California is as pure as you can get. And in fact, Maie's breathing and health did improve almost from the day we arrived in California.

Our move to California was one of the most important things we have done. It meant that Maie would live a long life.

While we were in Brecksville, I received a sad call that a good friend, Gardner Weeks, had died. He was the first of my contemporaries to pass on. We were in high school together, and in a good-mannered way, we were competitors in almost every way. He was always in a hurry. He finished his college degree in three years and couldn't wait to practice medicine.

I was deeply shaken when I got the call. He had lost control of his Volkswagen on a slippery Michigan road. He left a wife and two children.

Gardner was smarter than I could ever be. That didn't matter. Best of all, we had such good times together. We could laugh endlessly.

His funeral struck me so deeply that I shall never forget the event. It made me realize that he would no longer be here. He was gone. He was no longer a person. Somehow I couldn't quite fathom this. Gone meant gone. But I couldn't understand this.

The services were absolutely quiet. Gardner's father walked in. I had known him as a distinguished lawyer and a senior corporate executive at Glidden Corporation, a paint company. Now he was distraught and sunken. I was shocked. He had lost his son, and the depths of his despair showed. I walked with him to his car, and he burst into tears. I didn't know what to do or to say. I offered to drive him, as he didn't look in condition to drive anywhere. He declined and drove away. I will never forget that moment. All of his world had fallen. I felt what must have been only a small part of the moment. Little was I to imagine that I would someday be that man.

2 Months

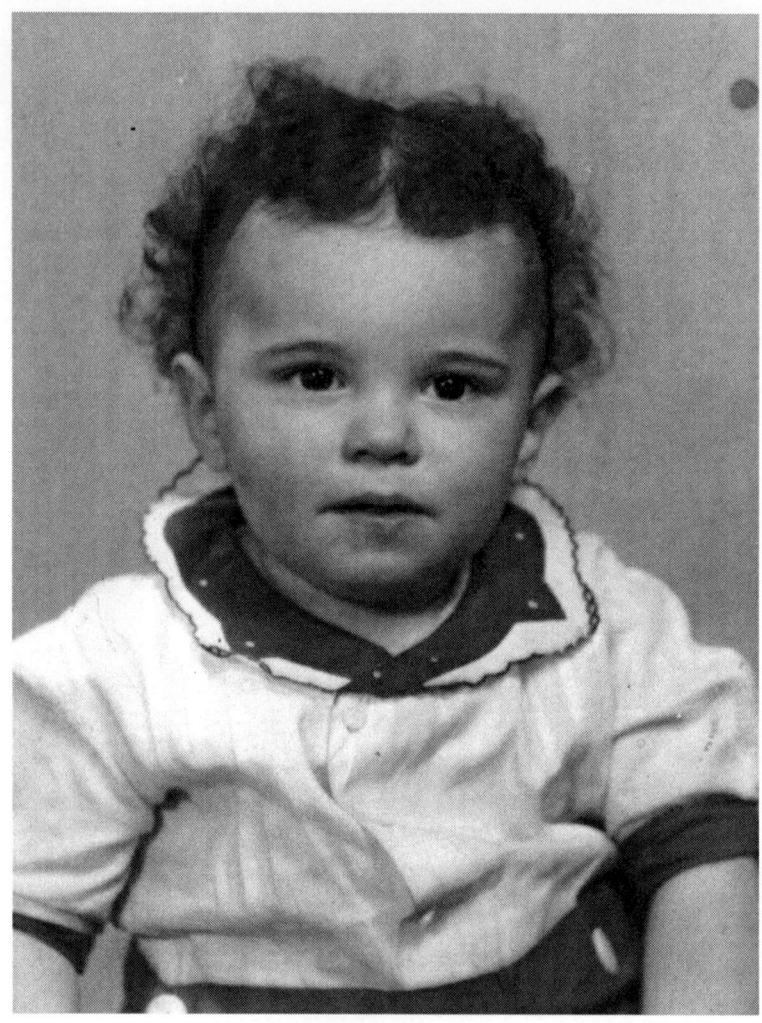

"What's going on out there?"
18 Months

A pensive moment
2 Years

Playing by Grandmother's abandoned Buick
5 Years

Out for a walk, Mother and myself
6 Years

Dad and myself
9 Years

Graduation from Columbia College
22 Years

Learning German, Mayerhofen, Austria
25 Years

Happy moment,
Maie and myself

Maie's mother, Hilde Kaarsoo, my father, Stanford Herrick,
my mother, Elizabeth McLaughlin, myself, Maie and Maie's
father, Alfred Kaarsoo, bottom, Maie's niece, Karin, 1963

Maie, Alan, myself and Sylvi, 1981

Top Dogs
Lou Bellucci, Manager New York Office, myself,
and Frank Baxter, Chairman, Jefferies & Co.

Northstar, California
Myself
57 Years

*Matthias, Sylvi, Maie, with Noora and Siena
in front. Shopping in a market, Rome.*

Enjoying a good laugh
The Chief and myself

Myself, Andrus Ansip, Maie, and Tiina, Andrus' daughter

Alan Kalev Herrick
October 28, 1970 - May 22, 1995

Sylvi taking a picture of Maie and me after receiving an award,
The Rose Garden of the Presidential Palace, Tallinn, Estonia

Chapter 13

Sylvi and Matthias

1967 to Present

Daughter, Sylvi, came into the world while we were in Brecksville. She has given me wondrous joy.

We come from nothing, and we return to nothing. But in between, we can shine forth our talents and give our love. Sylvi does these beautifully and naturally. She truly cares about me, I can tell.

I cannot imagine my life without her.

Having children did not start out auspiciously for Maie and me. During the initial four years of our marriage, Maie seemed to always be carrying a child for up to three months, and then the child was lost.

This is a hardship for a mother that is hard on the physical body and hard on the spirit. To lose a child time after time becomes a very discouraging way of living. But hooray for Maie. She never became discouraged.

So when Sylvi came into this world, we were quietly thankful in a way that other people were not aware. More than that—we were desperately thankful, if you can imagine what that feeling might be.

Maie delivered Sylvi without any complications. Her doctor was always confident, and he was right.

When we brought Sylvi home to Brecksville and put her into her crib, she was so tiny. I didn't realize new babies were so small. I looked at her in her crib, and she seemed barely breathing. She was motionless. Helpless. And so beautiful. I left the room and went into the living room. There was silence. I couldn't believe that there was no noise, no crying. Little did I realize what was to lie ahead.

The first tussle over Sylvi was over her name. We thought of many names—Linda was one—but we decided on Sylvi. I thought it was an Estonian name. Then came the question of how to spell that name. In the meantime, the hospital had given up asking us to spell her name and sent the official birth certificate over to the county with a blank space for her first name. We didn't know this, or we would have had a fit. But for her first six weeks, Sylvi did not officially have a first name.

Everyone had their own way of spelling Sylvi. Finally, something had to be done. I contacted the county and told them what we wanted the spelling to be. The clerk simply went to the records and handwrote her name on the birth certificate. So much for officialdom and formalities.

We gave her the second name of Anne after Maie's cousin

in Estonia. This cousin is one of the loveliest people in the family.

As Sylvi grew older, she became inquisitive about everything. She would pick up a simple thing like a stick and look at it. She loved to look at leaves. She always wanted to know what was what. You couldn't explain things enough for her.

She also became very sensitive to her surroundings. Her environment was important to her. If Maie and I were not as happy as we would have liked, she became disturbed. She wanted harmony and to be part of that peace.

When she was still very young, not even in school, she showed a remarkable sense of color. Her elementary school asked the second grade students to paint a picture on a large wall. All of the students took jars of paint and plastered on the paint. Sylvi mixed the paint into subtle shades. The most remarkable of these were pink and purple. These colors stood out as being beautiful just as they were.

She loved to challenge her friends. She would put Cathy Spitters or Amy Armstrong or sometimes Pam Ware on the handlebars of her bicycle and then blindfold them. She would pedal them to a part of Palo Alto they were not familiar with and set them free. The challenge was to find their way back to their home. She would follow them, laughing all the way at their befuddlement and her high jinx.

She loved to draw. And her drawings were happy drawings. She developed a type of cartoon that showed these happy figures dancing here and dancing there. I loved to see her drawings. They always cheered me up.

When Sylvi grew up, we had many wonderful occasions to share experiences. One important one was her application to college. This is a big moment for most high school seniors. Sylvi had applied to a half dozen of the prestige schools in the New England states. We had just arrived back from a skiing vacation when the replies from these schools were in the mail.

She took the envelopes, ran into her room, and shut the door. I waited for her to come out. When she did, she was in tears, sobbing. She said she had been turned down by every college she had applied to.

It took some time for me to look over the letters. When I did, I found one letter from Hamilton College had declined her admission in an outright manner but asked if she would like to be placed on the wait list in the event an opening might occur. That's all I needed. It was time for action.

I sat down with Sylvi and outlined a plan which I knew would work, and she would be going to this college in the fall. The plan was to go to every one she had contact with and to ask them to write a special letter of recommendation, given her current circumstances. Then we would talk with her school principal to see if he could speak to someone to get her admitted, at least to one of the University of California colleges. Finally, we would make a trip to Hamilton and ask for a personal interview.

She did all of this. But she didn't want to go to the University of California college that would be open to her. That didn't matter because her college of choice, Hamilton, still remained on the radar screen.

We arrived on campus, and Sylvi arrived at the soccer team practice and went out to the field to join the Hamilton team in a warm up. It turned out that the coach was impressed but never had received any notice that she had applied to the college. We straightened that out fast.

On the third day of our visit, and as the final step in our program, we received notice that she would have an interview by an admissions person. We arrived on time, and the lady who interviewed Sylvi, Mrs. North, invited her into her office and then turned to me and invited me to join them. I declined, because I wanted this to be only a meeting with Sylvi. Mrs. North persisted, so I agreed. As I sat down I said to myself that I would not say a word—at all.

All was going nicely, and then came the bombshell. Mrs. North turned to Sylvi and said, "Now tell me Sylvi, why are you here?" I knew that all rested on this answer. Sylvi said, "Mrs. North, I have been turned down by Hamilton and other colleges. Yet I very much want to go here, and I am on the wait list. I would hope you could admit me." Mrs. North said something, showed us the door, and we walked out. Sylvi couldn't wait to get outside to ask how things went.

We walked by a brook, and I told Sylvi that it appeared to me that Mrs. North had admitted her right on the spot. I said that she had been totally truthful, totally sincere, and that this is what I figured Mrs. North prized most of all in her life. That was my assessment of the situation and Mrs. North.

It worked. Ten days later Sylvi received a letter of admission. There was great joy in our house that day. The first thing she did was go into her room and, out of pure haste, slam the door shut. She then called her good friends, including Pam Ware, Kathy Spitters, and Amy Armstrong. Good news can't be shared quickly enough.

I told Sylvi she had just learned an important lesson in life—that there is no such thing as the word *no*.

Sylvi has always wanted to do things at the last minute. Sometimes this has led to some tight situations. She is still our girl, and we don't want anything to happen to her.

One day, she told us that she and Matthias, her husband, were going to take a trip to the Dominican Republic in the Caribbean. Sylvi needs vacations, I think, in order to survive.

This was a vacation that Matthias wanted, so he could practice his new sport of kite-boarding. It is a way of having a large kite pull you across the crests of the waves. It is really something to see.

They were to have been gone for five days, and Maie and I were to help look after the children. Sylvi casually mentioned that she had misplaced her United States passport, but she had a Euro passport from her citizenship of Estonia, which she received a few years ago by virtue of Maie's original Estonian citizenship. That didn't sound right to me, but I let it pass.

Then at five o'clock in the morning she was to leave, I woke up suddenly terrified. At that moment, this sounded like a trip to disaster. Since the attack on the World Trade Center, the immigration people had become sticklers for everything being just right at the borders. I imagined that when Sylvi presented the Euro passport, it would raise all sorts of flags.

The basis of the problem would be that she lived in the United States and that is where her passport should be from. Worst of all, my concern was that she would be denied reentry into the United States until she got a new United States passport. I waited until six o'clock and then woke her up and gave her this unhappy thought. It didn't go over, and she set off to meet Matthias.

Four days later, we received the dreaded phone call. Yes, Sylvi had been denied reentry, not by the immigration people, but by the airline, which wouldn't let her on the plane. Everything turned out all right in the end, and Sylvi got her passport in a remarkably short two days.

I love this story (and am sure that it is not one of Sylvi' favorites) because it illustrates two of the dominant patterns of her life. First, everything backs up to the last minute, and if loose ends are flapping in the breeze, that's okay. Second, Sylvi has an aura of good luck that surrounds her like a magic electric field. Bad things come her way but never get to her. I know this sounds silly, and in today's modern world, we don't believe that these things are possible. And I would never want to test this in any way. Let well enough alone. But there it is. It keeps happening.

Sylvi is beautiful. She was fortunate to have a background of family that was good-looking, and she inherited the best from both sides of her forbearers. In high school, she was popular with a wide circle of friends, from clubs to sports. In fact, in one instance she was voted the girl with the best-looking legs. Although she is now more than twice the age she was when she attended high school, her underlying beauty shines through.

Her principal sport was soccer. Nevertheless, after she graduated from Palo Alto High School, she also started to play frisbee, which in many ways is more difficult than soccer.

Sports were always an important part of her life. But it was sports that she could play that interested her, not the professional type that gets played in a large stadium and is reported in newspapers and television. Sylvi has to play the sport itself for it to interest her.

On a soccer field, she is a beautiful sight to behold. She always moves in a graceful manner. Her turns are like ballet. You get a sense that she is always in perfect balance and that nothing comes her way without her readiness to deal with it. This is apparent when she is observed in the field, but it becomes very clear when videos of her performance are viewed. I suppose the focus of a video gives this the clarity that is right up front.

She was good about passing the ball. Whenever there was a better position for a goal by someone else, Sylvi always passed. But whenever there was a good chance for Sylvi to add a point, Sylvi bore down and was accurate in getting the ball into the net. You might say Sylvi was an aggressive player. The coaches certainly thought so and always put her up front as the right striker.

Sylvi was beautiful to watch. Each motion was graceful. This was natural for her. She didn't practice art in motion. It was just the way she played.

Sylvi always played to win. There were none of the feelings of the loser. They simply didn't count. Her mother often spoke about how the losing team must feel. To Sylvi this was a nonevent. You aimed to win and let the chips fall where they may for those that were not winners. I always liked this attitude, especially when you were the winner.

But Sylvi was never dejected when the team lost. She usually told the team that if they played to their very best, there could be no regrets. That was the time to pick up the pieces and at a later time to figure out how to win in the next game. She was never down in the dumps after a game that turned out unfavorably. I admired that spunk and still do.

All of this was very important for Sylvi. She was regularly voted team captain or cocaptain in soccer in high school and college, so a lot of people were leaning on her to carry the day. The team captain carries more responsibilities than any other position. You must be a leader to do the job right.

Sylvi carried this responsibility easily on her shoulders. That too was a marvelous sight. I was very proud. I wanted to brag but resisted. If I had it to do over again I wouldn't be so resistant and would have gone ahead and bragged. After all, I'm her dad and am entitled to that privilege.

Sylvi's boyfriends—all of them—had an artistic talent of some kind. Often, they could play the guitar and sing a song. Sometimes they composed the song, and it was an original for Sylvi. I didn't appreciate this at first. The songs sounded a bit like they were from the same source, when I first heard them. How unobservant I was. These songs were equal to anything we could hear on television. It was my lack of perception that kept me in the dark.

I wish that I had recorded some of those songs. As I recall, her boyfriend Cub, for Kevin Donahue, wrote and sang the best of this unofficial collection. But all were very good.

I should add that there was a special spot in my heart for Cub. He was her boyfriend during much of her high school years, as I recall, and he always had a smile for me. But what made me appreciate him was my feeling that he would protect her from any harm that might come her way. I had a strong feeling this way. Proof that I was right was that we never heard of an incident that came close to a worry.

When the time came for Sylvi to get married, we were thrilled. She had traveled the world, and she decided it was time for the next stage in her life.

That time came when she was vacationing in the Yucatan peninsula, which is part of Mexico. She sat down at a bistro on the beach, and there, a few seats away, sat Matthias Herzog, her future husband—although she didn't know that at the time. They struck up a conversation and found they were meant for each other.

How wonderful it was that Sylvi brought Matthias into our lives. He is truly a remarkable person. Most of all, he is a very kind man. He is also a strong protector. It is rare to find these two qualities together, and yet they are both essential for a good husband.

In addition, Matthias is highly intelligent. He figures things out in his mind quickly. He thus avoids the mistakes that most people make in daily life by working things out as they go along.

Matthias has fitted into our family very nicely. And he has worked hard to build his new family. That takes a lot of work and dedication. He has done every bit of this work and then some.

There are many little stories of Matthias's thoughtfulness. Here is one. We needed a repair with our vacuum cleaner. I forgot exactly what the problem was, but a self-styled expert announced he would fix it. After half of an hour, he put the vacuum cleaner down, unable to do the job. After some time had passed, Matthias took the vacuum to another room and fixed it. But everything was done without notice, so as not to embarrass the first person. It was all done right.

Sylvi has considerable talent in mainstream art. But she is equally talented in modern art, including cartoons. Some of her best work is in this field. Her cartoons have a special touch—nobody can imitate them. They have an upbeat character and are quite simply original.

Once she made some T-shirts which she intended to sell

at a Grateful Dead concert. These were stenciled pictures of the performers in a stylized cartoon format that danced on the T-shirt. They were terrific.

She took them to the concert and sold several right away. Then the management of the concert confiscated the remainder, and she was left with none. But what a tour de force in commercial art!

When she was in high school, she got a job in a florist shop. She arranged flowers and delivered them. For a while, I thought she was going to open her own shop. She picked up the ways of the business fast; she was a natural for this business.

Our home was filled with day-old flowers, still in their prime, and the fragrance of the flowers perfumed each room. Having an abundance of flowers in a home is a wonderful way to live.

Alas, the job didn't last long, so that idea crashed. But it showed how deeply I was involved with what she would do. Watching her work with flowers made my eyes light up.

After Sylvi graduated from Hamilton College, she thought she might go into the clothing business as a designer or as a retailer. This looked like a reasonable course to take. It would include almost all of her talents and skills.

To get training in this field, she decided to attend the Fashion Institute of Design and Merchandising, which is located in San Francisco. Sylvi learned the skills of designing and cutting clothes, but I think she regarded this as a trade school and lacking in deeper aspects of work. There must be a philosophy behind what one does for Sylvi to be really satisfied. That wasn't part of that program.

In any event, the background gave her the credentials to apply for a sales position at Neiman Marcus at their San Francisco store, which is a premier retail store in the Bay Area. She was given a preferred location right at the start—ladies better dresses. This is the upgrade, but not ritzy, clothing where the store makes a large part of its profit.

During the first month, she did well. The second month, very well. And the third month, her sales were terrific. Then a slide took place, and she eventually left the store.

This was pure Sylvi. Her heart has to be in her work for her to pursue the next step. There was a lot of backbiting in the store, and customers can drive any sane person crazy. As a sales clerk, you have to take all of this on the chin, smile, and go after the next customer. It's a highly focused business.

This is not the way Sylvi wanted to spend her waking hours. Life meant something higher, in some nondescribed manner. Sylvi thought of herself as part of the unrecognized—can I say the word without sounding pretentious?—aristocracy. She felt she had a better background than what Neiman had to offer.

In keeping with a higher calling, Sylvi applied for a job in teaching, right after she graduated from Hamilton College— teaching English in Japan. Sylvi regarded this work as high on the totem pole, since she admired the Japanese culture. And she was in a position of authority, which appealed to her greatly.

She loved this work and formed many fast friendships with

the staff and students. She learned that she can be a very effective teacher, and her heart is in this mode of work. I was happy that she had this experience early in her career. All of her life, she will benefit from this knowledge of herself.

Sylvi did not stop with Japan when she traveled to the Far East. She went on to other countries, and one of my favorite pictures of her is one where she has a monkey on her shoulder, and the monkey is reaching out as if to swing to a branch. Both are having loads of fun, and it shows beautifully.

She ended this tour of exotic places in Perth, Australia. She made money as she went along, and she was entirely self-sufficient. In Perth, for example, she worked in a short-order eatery and rode a trolley to this place from where she lived. And this trolley went part of the way by the water. It was quite lovely.

There was a troubling moment during this year that she was away, and that was her health. She came down with some sort of stomach disorder, and she called us to tell us but also to tell us she was not so sick as to have us come to her.

One of the great regrets of my life was to have believed her. I should have put the phone down and gone directly to the airport and gotten on the next plane to where she was. She needed an advocate in that strange and distant country, and I should have been there with no discussion and no questions asked. Maie should have been with me too. It turned out okay, but that is not the answer. I will never forgive myself—but have learned, so that if there is a next time, I will know what to do.

Sylvi loves to teach art. Her teaching at California College of the Arts was a fine introduction. She was never quite sure that she fitted in at this college. It is never easy to be a student at a college and then return as a faculty member. You are always thought of in the lesser capacity.

That is not the case at Flagler College, where she is professor—or some such similar position—and comes from a highly regarded art school, as well as with an MFA, the credentialing degree.

Her classes invariably show more progress in their work than any other. And Sylvi dedicates more of her time to course work than anyone I know. Teaching will be increasingly her devoted work, I am sure. And what a fine profession.

Sylvi also keeps up with her special friends from Hamilton College, especially Megan Meyer, who teaches at the University of Maryland. Megan, I hear, would like to move with her husband close to Sylvi and Matthias. She also is close to Tracy Kinney, who lives in New York.

Thus, in addition to teaching, Sylvi loves to travel, as does Matthias. She enjoys travel in its simplest pleasures—walking down a street, looking in a window, observing how people cross a street. These are all things that people ordinarily do in a day. When Sylvi gets done observing them, they take on a higher meaning, an artistic transformation. That is the eye of an artist. Someday, I believe that Sylvi will put all of this together in some wonderful way.

I think Sylvi's interest in travel is inherent. But we

unknowingly contributed to it by taking our family on trips to faraway places while Sylvi and Alan were young. The first trip was to New York and Washington DC, followed by Sun River in Oregon, and Victoria Island and Palm Springs. The two were in their early teens. Then came Europe, China, Japan, Southeast Asia, and more of Europe. This was at a time when families seldom made such extensive trips. Sylvi adored these trips and still remembers incidents that I had long forgotten.

Sylvi became serious about education and teaching when she enrolled in the master of fine arts degree program at California College of Arts. It was an enriching, but at times difficult, session. Sylvi does not like to be commanded by authority, and any educational institution has a share of these people on its faculty and staff. But the benefits far outweigh these personnel tiffs. Most of all, Sylvi earned the terminal degree in fine arts and has credentials among the best in the world. That is so important today, and it will be more so in coming years.

I would expect some disagreement in an art school. Artists are supposed to feel passionately about their work and get heated up by self-appointed experts, as well as proclaimed experts. It's all part of the game. Sylvi fits in just right. The difference is that Sylvi produces original art and, through her personality and teaching skills, gets others to go beyond themselves and also produce outstanding art.

Sylvi could be practical. We gave her a one-half interest in a house in Oakland, not far from California College of the Arts. It was broken down and in terrible shape when she got it. The idea was to fix up the house and sell it. The profit would be hers. Well, after she fixed it up, it was too nice to sell, so we kept it, and she lived in it. She lavished it with lovely touches. The most outstanding was to make it a house of flowers—everywhere. Her plantings were astounding.

When Sylvi and Matthias decided to move to St. Augustine, the house went up for sale. In a terrible real estate market, the house sold in a matter of weeks, confounding everyone. I am sure the reason was the flowers and little touches.

Then in St. Augustine, she is doing the same thing to the house that they bought—except everything is on a larger scale. This house is on its way to become also the most beautiful home on the street.

Maie and I are very happy and grateful that Sylvi and Matthias would like us to be closer to them and to their daughters, Noora Pearl and Siena Jade. We feel that we are specially privileged that we are wanted. Noora Pearl with her graceful demeanor and flowing blond hair, and Siena Jade with her brown hair with a tinge of red and intense, magnetic personality. We told them my name was Pops. They renamed me Popsie. A great improvement and I'm in bliss for it all.

We are now building a small house next to their home. We would then have a place that would be close, but not right on top of their family. I think it will work out nicely.

Sylvi deeply loved her younger brother, Alan. From the time they were little, and Sylvi dragged him from his bed to read him early morning stories, to the time they spent talking about life and how to live the right way, they were inseparable. She organized and ran his birthday parties which were peak events of the year for everybody. She dressed him as a bunny and a ballet dancer and made little stage plays with him as the hero.

When they grew older, they looked after each other. They were soul mates. Alan is now gone. No one misses Alan more than Sylvi.

Chapter 14

Alan

1970 to 1995

As when we were throwing snowballs back and forth,
Roaring down the long and broad slopes,
What elation and prankish fun it was,
Can't this go on and on, forever, one hopes.

I miss you so, dear Alan,
What can I possibly do to undo it all,
My answer comes up as stark silence,
As somehow I must stand, as you must fall.

It was another usual Sunday night. The weekend had come and gone. Maie and I had taken a long walk during the day, and we were ready for bed. Alan had called us from Tahoe, where he had been skiing. He went to great lengths to thank us for all we had done for him, through the years, as he was growing up. He said that he wanted to tell us how much he loved us and how we had given him everything he needed and he was debt free.

I didn't know how to accept all of this praise, and I told him something like he deserved all he received because he worked at it. But he kept going. In the end, I felt good that we were appreciated then forgot about it.

It was time to call it a day, and I fell asleep watching the CNN news.

At three fifteen in the morning, the phone rang. Maie answered it and woke me up. "They called and said a policeman is at the door," she said.

"Policeman?" I said. "Who would want us at this hour?"

I put on a robe and tried to tie the belt and went to the front door. Sure enough, two policemen stood in blue uniforms. I opened the door.

"Mr. Herrick?" the policeman nearest me said. "It is my sad duty to tell you that your son has been killed in an auto accident."

I will never forget those words—that moment.

I knew, somehow, that this horror was true.

Maie gasped. "No no no, it can't be!"

As I think back, I feel sad for the policemen. This must be one of the most difficult tasks they do. They stand by, helpless, as two parents disintegrate into wails.

This was the darkest moment of my life. My precious son was no more.

I never thought this could happen. From time to time, I let

my mind wander, and the thought would come to mind—what might happen to Alan, could something unfortunate happen? My mind never let me go there. I just couldn't think about that.

Those thoughts were blocked by two things.

First, Alan was a terrific swimmer. He had, in fact, won an All American award in swimming in his senior year at Palo Alto High School. Why this would keep him safe, I don't know. But that's the way my mind worked.

Second, he was very lucky, in so many ways. I suppose I felt he would always be protected. How wrong I was.

My thoughts would sometimes settle on how he would take leadership in our family.

This didn't mean that Sylvi would take second fiddle. She would be the power behind the throne and figure out how things should go. Her leadership would be more intuitive. She would see around corners as to what would be coming.

But Alan would take active leadership. I felt that he would gain cooperation among the members of the family, including those yet to come. Like Sylvi, he had been cocaptain of his team—in his case, it was water polo; and in hers, it was soccer. Alan loved to play water polo. This is basketball in the water. You have to be able to throw a large ball with accuracy as well as swim like a fish. He was so expert at this. In fact, he perfected it to an art.

One of his best friends in high school was Cam Steele, also a water polo player and cocaptain of the team. Another was Steve Apfelberg. Steve always looked out for Alan. One time,

Alan was invited to an awards ceremony in his senior year. There were almost fifty awards for distinguished service, outstanding achievement, and helpfulness to the school. When the awards were completed and Alan had received nothing, he was greatly disappointed. In fact, he was crushed.

I was there and felt that he might prefer to be with his friends, who had gathered around him.

Wrong. He wanted to see me. It was Steve who left that group and came over to see me. He told me how badly Alan felt and that I was needed. It took Steve's presence of mind to let me know. I should have been with Alan right from the beginning. But it was better to be late than not be there at all. I talked with Alan about the whole situation, and I can't recall that I said anything very helpful. Being there was all that I really offered. Of all his friends, I believe Sandy Spector helped Alan the most. Sandy had a way of feeling your pain just as you did. Sandy felt Alan's pain.

The thought keeps coming back that Alan was an outstanding swimmer. The thought has always been at the forefront of my thinking. There was something important about that. Somehow, I felt that was the key to his role in the future of our family. Maybe it was the basic element of water that was in my mind.

Anyway, I felt he would be the one who would keep our family together as time went on, as Maie and I would take second fiddle.

A little event which occurred in Spain was one of the many times I was reminded of this.

Alan, Sylvi, Maie, and I were traveling in the hottest part of the summer in the hottest part of Spain; and our car, due to my oversight, did not have air-conditioning. Earlier in the day, Sylvi had been overcome by the heat. We stopped to buy a bag of ice, which we wrapped in plastic, and she put this miniature iceberg on her lap. We also drove through a raging brush fire which straddled the highway.

We arrived at our parador in Carmona, which was an old castle on top of a hill that had been converted into a hotel. The pool next to the hotel was just what we wanted, and we were before the edge in no time at all.

Alan paused for a moment as he surveyed the length of the pool, which must have been fifty meters or more. He dived into the water, leaving virtually no splash. With one breath, he swam under the water to the end and back without disturbing the water's surface. It seemed effortless, so smooth. So right.

My mind wandered. Then it settled. I thought that Alan had the grace and control to be our leader, when the time came. I was so glad that we had Alan.

Alan could also push his luck. Yet he always had come out ahead. He always seemed to win. Even when the odds were clearly not in his favor, he would come out on top.

He did this on an occasion when he was in very serious danger, at Washington and Lee University, and probably many other times I didn't know about.

Here is the incident. In his senior year at college, Alan shared a house on the Maury River with four other friends. His room overlooked the river, which flowed from the Blue Ridge Mountains to the Atlantic Ocean. The house was located about one-quarter of a mile from a high dam. Near the house, the river resembled an ordinary lake with a gentle current running through it. His window overlooked the water, and he loved it.

I did not see Alan's close call in this water. I learned about it by overhearing a conversation among his friends. When I asked Alan about it, he turned away. His friends did not want to talk about it, so I knew there was something important that was being kept from me.

The best that I could gather was that there was a spring party at the house where he lived, which followed a storm and heavy rain. Everyone was in good spirits.

Outside, the river had suddenly swollen. Instead of being calm, the water in the river was active and the current moved swiftly through it.

For some reason or no reason or just feeling the attraction of the powerful force of nature, Alan walked out to the river and went swimming. He moved in a vector course, heading in a direction that was both upstream and across the river. For a while, he kept about the same point where he had left the shore.

However, when he approached the middle of the river, he was caught in powerful undercurrents that enveloped him and swept him rapidly downstream toward a dam. The fall of the dam is about fifteen feet with rocks at the bottom.

Alan must have sensed he went too far and tried to turn

around. His efforts failed him. He rapidly approached the dam. He must have become alarmed and pressed himself to his limit.

He apparently saw a broken tree that extended into the water. It was his only escape. He caught hold of the tree's farthest branch. He held, and it held. The tree would have been one of the many that had recently been blown over by the rainstorm, and its branches were still supple.

I imagine that when Alan took his first step on land, he must have felt enormous gratitude. He had made it. He had challenged nature, winning where there would have been no second chance. It must have been a heady moment. One that gave him confidence that he could beat the odds, anywhere, anytime.

Alan applied to six graduate schools of film, and he was admitted to one of them, California College of Arts. This is the same school that Sylvi also attended several years later.

He had not studied film previously at Washington and Lee University, and he had taken only one art course. This was a humble beginning. In California, many young people grow up making videos, writing film scripts, and working with all kinds of electronic equipment. Alan wasn't in that league when he started film school. He also started at an advanced school, since he enrolled at the graduate level, aiming to receive a master's degree in fine arts.

Even with an exceptional background, many applicants for graduate film programs apply for several years in succession before they are admitted. The admissions people at the California College of Arts must have seen a spark in Alan. The letter notifying him of his admission carried a note next to the signature of the admissions director, Stephen Goldstine, which read, "Nice going, Alan."

Alan had just begun to find his way in film school when he reapplied to the Stephen A. Jefferies Educational Grant Program for a continuation of his scholarship. He had won a scholarship earlier. The application for the scholarship included a request for a description of his hopes and plans. Alan's response was unvarnished, yet brimming with hope. Here it is:

> "When I entered my first year of graduate studies at California College of Arts last fall, I had limited film experience, almost no knowledge of film equipment, and a basic knowledge of film history and theory.
>
> I was accepted to the school after submitting a portfolio of written work, slides of photography and painting, and one short video tape. I entered a school that has an unstructured program, where each person makes his own class schedule, and it is assumed that you will initiate your own work and the faculty helps you however they can. The film community at California College of Arts is small, and the film program does not offer many classes, but encourages students to

create their own classes through independent studies with faculty.

I had a difficult first semester.

After a few months, though, I became more comfortable and I took control of my situation. By the end of the school year I was able to operate four different video cameras, numerous professional quality video editing systems, as well as computer aided editing and graphics programs.

I learned more than just equipment. I was exposed to more than just equipment. I was exposed to a wide variety of film critique, art history, world history, postmodernist theory, and other stimulating readings, including readings by John Cage, Jean Baudrillard, Walter Benjamin, and many others. I saw all types of film, such as experimental work by Man Ray, Maya Deren, Ernest Gehr, documentaries, narratives and foreign work. I saw performance artists, video artists, sound composers and arrangers.

The school may lack a strong sense of conventional narrative, or Hollywood cinematic tradition, but it has exposed me to artists and styles and genres of art that I had never known about.

In addition to the training in equipment and education in critical thought, I learned by creating my own work. I produced one video, a twenty minute piece (which I would have submitted to the committee in my accompanying portfolio, but watching the piece would ruin my application's anonymity), one sound piece and shot one film.

The sound piece is an arrangement where I recorded the sounds of BART, a subway, and sampled or fragmented the sounds into short bits, and looped, or repeated the sounds, and then arranged and mixed them into a classically structured piece of industrial sounds.

The film that I shot took a semester of work just to write, produce and shoot, and I am still only two-thirds of the way there. I have an hour's worth of black and white 16 mm film to edit, optically print, and finish into a piece that will be about fifteen minutes long. It took three full days to shoot over two locations and I had a twelve person crew to direct. The film will eventually cost me two thousand dollars.

Raising money for a film is very difficult, but it is the reality for anyone who wishes to be an independent filmmaker, which is my long term goal. But learning how to save money is just as important as learning how to obtain it. I am discovering ways of both raising funds and cutting costs, and I have confidence that I will be successful in both.

Being an independent filmmaker appeals to me because it combines business and art in a unique way. I love the creativity and organization that filmmaking requires, and I am interested in the entrepreneurial nature of fundraising, or producing a film. Whoever funds the production has the final word on its content, which is why I want to work for myself and be an independent.

Film is expensive, so being an independent means working with a comparatively small budget and turning to grants, donations and whatever other forms of financial aid one can find in order to help make a film.

But there are ever increasing opportunities to make films. The most high profile and potentially profitable way is to become involved in the Hollywood industry, work for a major studio and create multi-million dollar commercial films. One can make industrial films, in which case the sponsor would be a large corporation, such as General Motors, and make promotional films. Large corporations also sponsor documentaries, as seen on public television.

The entertainment industry is exploding. Fiber optic cable access means that soon the cable companies will be able to send signals through phone lines, and there will be 500 cable stations. Interactive media and high definition television are exciting and threatening to explode in an industry which is already the United States' third largest grossing export industry.

The entertainment and electronic communications media industry boom is just beginning. There are many people with creative ideas, but who will know how to use the technology and equipment to communicate these ideas through film, video and or computer software (these three media are merging).

I appreciate the committee's time in considering my application, and I very much look forward to learning of your decision."

That was a truly remarkable letter, one that I will always treasure.

I can't help it, but I keep coming back to the tragedy, even though more than fifteen years have elapsed.

In the car with Alan was Paul Winkler, his best friend at Washington and Lee College, as well as California College for the Arts. They often went on bicycle rides together and went on trips together. The car was Paul's, an Acura coupe, a sporty car. They had debated whether or not to take Alan's van or the Acura. The Acura had no insurance on it. In fact, Maie and I paid Paul for the loan that remained on the car after the accident.

Maie and I always liked Paul. He was a good friend to Alan as well as to us. Yet Alan had never driven that car prior to the fateful accident, and that was not the time for him to have done so. On this subject, much more could be said, but I believe that I should let that discussion lie in peace.

Alan's greatest talent was that he was a consummate writer. He did many outstanding things, but writing was by far his strongest.

He was just beginning to realize this when his life ended. But I saw it many years earlier.

He was in high school and had worked on a report for some time, and he asked me to look it over. I sat down and was ready to give it a tough review. I read it once, twice, three times and could find virtually nothing to suggest. I was impressed and told him it was a good job, ready to turn in. He thanked me and took the report back.

Later that evening, he handed me the report back again. I couldn't believe it. He had revised it again, and the report was even better than before. I have never had that happen in any other circumstance. I was impressed.

This talent was inside him and had just begun to be developed.

Sometimes I let my mind wonder, and I think about what Alan might have done. But my mind doesn't want to go there. It just won't do that. It is too painful. Tears come to my eyes when I do. I just stop. That's all there is.

There were never any moments when I was truly angry with Alan. He wasn't that kind of boy or young man. He never got spanked by me. I just couldn't do that. I always felt he was more hurt than I was upset whenever things didn't go right.

We always liked his girlfriends. He went with Duffy Ross in high school. She was a quiet companion, with a ready smile for us. We couldn't see enough of her. Alan didn't bring her by our house very often.

In college and afterward, he went out with Tracy Kinney, who was also a close friend of Sylvi's. In fact, they went on a trip to Mono Lake just a week before the tragedy. We got to know Tracy's family and enjoyed many happy moments with her mother, father, and brothers. They continue to be friends of ours.

Tracy, Alan, and I sometimes would have an outing, and these events were always fun. It was fun just to be with them too. One event was the annual dog show at the Cow Palace. We watched the showing and saw all of the beautifully groomed pets and would always comment on how much the owners looked like the dogs. We laughed a lot. After that show, I should have taken everybody to a late lunch but for some reason didn't. It's strange how that omission sticks in my mind. It's a reminder to always do things completely and not to let an opportunity slip by. Now I know.

A trying moment was when I bought a new bicycle for myself. It was a dark grey beauty. Maie believes that the bicycle was really hers, but that doesn't matter to the story. I had just parked it in the garage—yet to take it for a spin—when Alan asked if he could ride it. Of course, I handed it over to him.

He took the bicycle to a football game at Stanford, locked the bike with a chain, and went to the game. When he came out, the chain had been cut, and the bicycle was gone. He came to me to tell me the bad news. I couldn't get mad at him. I knew he felt terrible.

One of his happiest moments was when he played the part of Superman in a high school amateur night. He got dressed up in a Superman suit and strode onto the stage in just enough of a touch of ham acting that brought the house down. I don't think he ever got over that magnificent moment. I couldn't stop laughing for the rest of the evening. I was also very proud of him that he could laugh at himself so easily.

I wanted him to have a good suit when he turned sixteen. Alan didn't like suits. They reminded him of the stuffy establishment that he didn't want to be connected with. He felt comfortable being among the establishment, but he didn't want to be considered as one of them.

So I told him we would find a personal tailor, and we wouldn't go to a fancy establishment store. With reluctance, he agreed. I found the retired tailor of Brooks Brothers, and we went to his home and he prepared the suit. It turned out to be just perfect. But Alan went out of his way not to wear that suit. I tried.

Perhaps the most difficult remembrances were where I did not help him as much as I could have done.

When he was twelve years old, he entered a track competition. One of the races was jumping over hurdles. Alan never had the training he needed for this. I knew this but, at the time, was just starting new work with Jefferies & Co. Inc., and was busy with this work. Alan's grandfather, Isa, quickly looked after him and built some hurdles out of scrap wood. He then coached Alan how to run and jump over these hurdles.

I sat in my office, pouring over the materials before me, thinking that I should be outside with Alan, helping him. I knew hurdles more than his grandfather, and I should have been there right beside him. Well, I wasn't and felt terrible about it. There is no question that I made the wrong choice.

But there were many right choices. And I am grateful for every one of them.

Our skiing trips were always the right choice. The best times were when Alan and Sylvi would ski along with me. They were ordinarily good skiers but had not developed into the cracker jack skiers they were to become. We would go down the slopes together, talking about this and that, and then I would see some fresh snow, just right for making snowballs. They would then go ahead, and I would make an arsenal of half a dozen of these snow balls, catch up with them, and start a snowball fight while skiing.

This was not a great thing to be proud of—in fact, it was pretty much a dangerous thing to do. But under the impulse of the moment, it seemed like the perfect thing to do. Well, they loved it, scooped their own snowballs from the snow, and we laughed at each hit we made. Their mother knew nothing of this, since she was on the bunny slope, making snowplow turns. Being a bit naughty with your kids is always great fun.

What I am about to describe is difficult to believe. But it is completely true.

Alan died on the night of May 22, 1995. One week earlier, I had a dream that I will never forget. In the dream, I saw a macadam road, and there were tall pine trees in the distance. It was night time, yet there was enough light to see the road and trees. A vehicle that looked like an emergency truck was to my left. It was painted a light color. Its rear doors faced me, and it had lettering on it, but I do not recall what it said. There was no car visible. Immediately before me was a stretcher covered with a white sheet, and I knew that nobody was underneath this sheet. To my right, a little farther away, was another white sheet. I knew that Alan was under that sheet, and I knew that he was dead.

I awoke terrified. The dream remained clearly in my mind. I got out of bed, went to get a glass of water, and returned to bed. I dozed off, and the dream returned just as vividly as before. This time, I lay in bed awake until morning.

Subsequently, I learned from the police that the dream showed the exact scene of the accident. The car that Alan drove did not appear in the dream, since it had fallen over the side of the road, landing in the Truckee River, ten feet below the road. Everything was as it would be nine days later.

I do not understand how these things are possible. It is as if our lives are somehow written out before us and that we simply live out the part that has been given to us. The whole idea of past, present, and future would be somehow meaningless; there would only be one dimension, that of the present, where all would be combined. But whatever would be the case, there was some reason that I would have this dream. I wish I knew what that reason might be. I have not been able to figure it out.

I cannot describe the feeling that the loss of a child brings to a parent. There is nothing like it. It is profound loss, way beyond anything else in life. And it is a feeling of helplessness where one is at sea with waves that never cease. The only way to survive is through the gift of closeness of one's spouse, children, family, loved ones, and friends. They held me up, and they continue to hold me up. And I am so deeply grateful. I cannot ever give enough thanks to them.

Chapter 15

Palo Alto

1970 to Present

I started my work at Stanford Research Institute in the final week of September 1970. It was with the long-range-planning group, which had just been relocated to the new International Building. This was a beautiful, new white building and the most attractive place where I had ever worked.

The immediate manager of this operation was Doug Hurd, and the overall director was Richard Funkhouser, who had an office a bit farther away, and the big chief was Ken Beggs, who was vice president of the institute. So I was a small fish in the overall organization.

But I had been chosen for a reason. The institute did not have a credentialed economist, and Ken Beggs very much felt he needed one to do the things he had in mind. Basically, he hoped to expand what was broadly referred to as the economics sector of the institute. I was to be the point man. I was placed in the long-range-planning group to give me time to get acclimated to the institute.

While all of this was going on, Maie gave birth to Alan. I can still see her window at Stanford Hospital where she stayed for a few days. I always have a lump in my throat as I look up at that window. Our family now included two beautiful children, we had just relocated to a part of the world that was beautiful beyond belief, and I had come full circle back to working as an economist.

I didn't have my feet on the ground, but I was happy. People—all people—were very helpful, and everybody seemed to sense that we seemed to be new at West Coast living.

Maie's old friend, Tina, had arranged rental of an attractive three-bedroom house on a side street in the middle of Palo Alto. We paid two-hundred-ninety-five dollars rent per month, and the house had everything one could hope for.

Maie was soon wrapped up in looking after Sylvi and Alan. She managed to do so much so effortlessly. But she had help from visitors, her mother and father and my mother and later from Ruth Albin. Ruth looked after Alan like a devoted nanny. So the house hummed as diapers got changed, and everybody took little walks down the sidewalk. The sidewalks were luxuries we had not enjoyed when we were living in Brecksville.

This is how we settled in. We found our place in this new land, which was still largely cut off from the mainstream of America. By Christmas, we realized we wanted to live here for all of our years. It was our paradise. I knew this as soon as I discovered oranges on a tree outside my window.

Not everyone felt that way, however. Sylvi missed her nanny back in Ohio, Nanty Nable, which was her pronunciation of Aunt Mable. One day, she took a hammer from the garage and started banging on the house. Maie and I ran over to her and asked her what in the world she was doing. She was three and a half at the time. She said she was breaking down this new house so she could go back to the old house.

We noticed a change in our diet. In the Midwest, we ate steak and roast beef as a delicacy and served meats to honored guests. We never served fish to guests, except perhaps salmon to international friends. And we ate ourselves in this preference. Meat loaf and lots of buttered potatoes with rich gravy ladled to the brim. There were few vegetables, and they were often cooked to the end of time. Fruits were for picnics.

The opposite was the case in Palo Alto. It was fish and pasta, with tons of vegetables nobody in the Midwest had ever heard of. All cooked only a little, so they were a little bit raw. Even fish was sometimes eaten raw. No rich gravies.

The Palo Alto diet took a little time to get used to, but in the end, the superior chefs did their work so well that we actually preferred the Western way of eating. All of this was for health in the end. It also had to do with eating what was supposed to be a more natural diet, whatever that meant.

Best of all, there was room for ice cream with both diets.

And the very best of the best of all were the new ice creams, frozen yogurts, sorbets, and other delights that were being developed all of the time. What a time to be alive!

There were some difficult moments with our family guests. In one instance, my mother kept smoking inside the house. I wasn't happy with this. Mother knew that but kept smoking, filling the house with fumes. I didn't know what to do. Then I got the bright idea of turning on the kitchen fan, to draw out the smoky air.

Mother caught on to my ploy and, in her aggressive way, confronted me with what I had done. I said that all she said was true but also added, "Would Mother please stop smoking inside the house?" The next morning, Mother packed her bags, and she and her husband, Barney, left in a huff. So sometimes, there were less than joyful moments. But they were few and far between.

Maie and I decided that we should ride bicycles to explore Palo Alto and Menlo Park. We did buy two dark green bicycles for thirty-nine dollars each, and we rode them together with the children on occasion. These were wonderful trips, and we toured the great variety of homes in this area. They ranged from magnificent palaces to small, no, smaller than small extended houses. Maie still has her green bicycle after all of these years. Mine was stolen years ago.

We decided that we should buy a home somewhere near Stanford Research Institute. We spoke with many realtors and finally bought our home at 1150 University Avenue from a smooth-talking gentleman, Mark Schmitz. We paid fifty-three thousand five hundred dollars, and we were scared to death that we were buying over our head. My income was twenty thousand dollars per year, and that was five thousand dollars less than I earned in Cleveland. Maie was at home, so my income had to cover everything, which was fine. The calculations said we should be all right, but still, we didn't know how all of our expenses would total.

Here we were, working for a decade, I was almost forty years old, and we were still feeling that we were on shaky ground. It wasn't supposed to be that way, everybody would tell us. We should be well on our way to the American dream. I began to think there might be something missing in that dream.

The house we bought was on a busy street, but it had a large back yard. Actually, it was a beautifully landscaped backyard with center grass to play on. And the garden had several lemon trees, several grapefruit trees, a large orange tree, apricot trees, a fig tree, a peach tree, and more. I was fascinated by the tropical fruit. I couldn't imagine being able to go outside in the morning and pick my oranges and squeeze them for juice. I couldn't believe that the people here took this for granted. To me, it was a fantastic gift.

The house was nondescript, as I first saw it. It had a flat roof and almost looked as if it was afraid of itself. It was painted ivory on the outside, and inside it was painted dark green. This was the same color that our house in Brecksville was painted. And I did the same thing in Palo Alto that I did in Brecksville.

I bought buckets of white interior paint and went from room to room, painting the walls and then the ceiling. It took a month of steady work every night and all of the free time on weekends.

What a difference the white paint made. An old friend, Tom Brandt, was once in the home resale business and would often comment that painting the interior of a house white would make it sell more rapidly and sell for 10 percent more than otherwise or sometimes even more. He was right in Brecksville, and it certainly made the house in Palo Alto more cheerful as well as much lighter.

That brought out the effects of an abundance of windows, which let in huge quantities of light from the outdoors. A white interior also is a cheerful color to look at during the long nights of winter.

To my surprise, springtime was much more than an abundance of flowers and blooms. It was also fragrances. A magnolia tree with purple blossoms as large as grapefruits filled the air with a heady, rich fragrance. The orange blossoms blanketed the rear porch. These pungent and spicy smells were heaven-sent.

The other unexpected gift was that there were virtually no mosquitos. The dry air, lack of rain for most of the warm months, and cool nights kept them at bay. What a wonderful relief from Ohio, where these pests were a constant battle.

I drove our 1966 Buick Skylark two-door car from Brecksville. It took five days and was a long but pleasant trip.

We had the other car, a Skylark four-door, driven over the same route. It cost one hundred dollars for the delivery, and except for some minor repairs along the way, both cars arrived safely.

We subsequently bought three more of these Skylarks. We bought a 1965 coupe for Maie, another one which we gave to Alan in his senior year at high school—and which was stolen from our driveway—and a 1964 four-door, which was smashed in a freeway accident where we were not injured.

I then bought a 1967 Oldsmobile 224, which was as close to a sports car as Detroit could get, at least for a production car. Alan was four when I made this purchase, and he loved to stand up by the console and fall asleep looking out of the window.

Jefferies & Co. gave me my choice of a car when I was appointed a director. I chose a 1983 Cadillac coupe, metallic red with a white top. The car had many problems, and Maie lost control on the freeway. I sold it five days later.

Then came an Acura coupe, a Honda four-door, and finally a Nissan four-door and an Infiniti four-door. The Japanese cars kept getting better as we went along. The American cars went downhill from the mid-1960s. The Americans literally gave away their franchise in dominating the automobile business, and it was a sad thing to watch. Nevertheless, things may have now changed. I hope so. But the Japanese cars have become awfully good.

We made friends through the Congregational Church which we joined. We joined this church because we had been members of this denomination back in Brecksville, and we liked the unpretentious way of the membership. Although we had received high-level educations—and some might describe as being elite—we never felt that we were something special. In my case, I was always concerned that I could keep everything together. I never felt entitled to anything. I was grateful to be able to keep going.

I had carried through this attitude for all the years we had been married. In fact, when we were first married, I bought a one-hundred-thousand-dollar insurance annuity from Canadian Premier Insurance Company, and 30 percent of my income went to pay for this policy. It promised to pay me over six hundred dollars per month when I retired, which was a lot of money in those days.

This annuity turned out to be the worst investment I ever made. The inflation of my working years washed away most of the buying power. If I had simply bought stocks or a stock mutual fund, I would have accumulated a sizeable sum. As it turned out, the monthly annuity bought little.

So we fitted into the California scene quickly and with good feelings about where we were. That was good.

From the moment I walked in the door at Stanford Research Institute, I was given a warm welcome and a feeling of respect. It was a well-ordered place. Gentlemanly conduct was universal. There was a feeling that there was great knowledge in the organization, a wonderful environment, but not necessarily a lot of money.

Doug Hurd greeted me and showed me my office. It was on the second floor and overlooked a lovely courtyard. I thought that I might make more money someday, but I would never be in a more hospitable and beautiful location. I also asked myself why I had not known of this place before.

Doug had gone to the graduate business school at Columbia University. I suspect that my attending the college and graduate faculty of economics was a connection that he regarded as being important. The old school tie must have worked in this case.

Columbia is an Ivy League school, and there were and still are very few Ivy League economists. In a consulting arrangement, that carried weight, although it was never discussed as an issue or advantage. And Oxford carried a mystique. So I gathered that I might have been viewed as a bit of a showpiece. That never bothered me. Anything that worked was good enough.

The long-range-planning group included about fifteen people who wrote articles for a publication. The group also held annual meetings in San Francisco for the clients. There were approximately 170 clients. Members of the group also visited clients, and a marketing man made the rounds to visit clients on a regular basis.

This planning group attempted to educate American businesses on how to plan ahead. Most companies thought planning was a good idea but had no idea of how to do it or what the benefits might be. I now regard planning as a reconstituted socialist product and a copy of what was openly practiced in communist countries. It is based on the assumption that the future can be controlled with information of some kind or other. This is a faulty assumption.

The future cannot be deciphered, no matter how good the information might be. The circumstances that form the future are simply unpredictable.

But in that earlier time, nobody had reached that conclusion. The logic of formulating the future in a business situation was too persuasive. This logic was not, of course, logic. But it was thought to be at the time.

I had two assignments given to me in my first week. First, I was asked to prepare a long-range-planning booklet on gross domestic product.

The idea was to make the report simple enough, so that anyone could understand it, yet also provide some insights that would be useful to economic analysts. I traveled to the University of Maryland which was at the time the leading light in this work and reviewed a work by Professor Almon and prepared the report, only to find out that the big chief, and vice president of the institute, Ken Beggs, shot it down.

I never got a chance to look into the subject of gross domestic product from another very interesting and potentially very important point of view. That was what I thought could be called sustainable gross domestic product. This concept would consider the environmental and other related costs to produce something. These costs would be subtracted from the sales price of the product or service. The result would be what the product or service actually cost from a broader social point of view.

The knowledge of these costs would be crucial for tax policy, as well as environmental regulation or elimination of regulation.

It was a whole new scheme of things, which had not been thought through at the time.

I later thought this project had the potential of a senior level of recognition, possibly a whisper of a Nobel Prize. Recognitions of this stature had been given for less.

I should have pursued the idea, but I didn't. It was one of those roads I didn't go down, unfortunately.

Nevertheless, when I saw Ken Beggs, he wasn't disturbed and asked me to take on a new consulting assignment.

This was with O'Melveny & Meyers, which was the premier law firm in Los Angeles. The assignment involved a challenge to the usury laws in California. At the time, there were laws preventing interest charges above a certain rate, and the lawyers were trying to use a special definition of interest in order to get around that law. The assignment was never finished and was dropped.

That was followed by work for the Office of Price Administration. This was work I was never proud of.

President Richard Nixon established this agency as part of his erstwhile program of price controls in order to stop inflation. I got involved when Ken Beggs sailed into my office one day and announced that I had just been appointed as price czar for iron and steel products.

One month before, I had been transferred to the economics group—I was the only economist in the group—and with it came a much larger office. I was also promoted to senior economist, which was nice.

I said to Ken that this was ridiculous. Price controls never work, and they never will work, and getting our names tied up with it would not be a very good idea. Ken laughed and said that the program would never last long and not to worry about that.

In the meantime, he said that there would be consulting fees from the government, and to get to work.

My enthusiasm was not with this project, and I had a hard time applying myself to making a determination of what the price of, for example, a ton of cold-rolled steel might be. Nobody seemed to care what price I put down. The reason was that nobody in the business world paid any attention to Mr. Nixon's price-control policy.

After two months, the project was dropped. But not before some possible large fees were piled up.

Then I worked on a long-range-planning report on the investment banking industry. This report hit the jackpot. Everybody wanted to be on board.

The work took me to interview the leading investment bankers in New York City, and in doing this, I carried the flag of Stanford Research Institute right into the heart of the investment-banking industry.

There must have been favorable comment of the work because Ken Beggs called me one day for an after-dinner meeting at the Institute. He said that Merrill Lynch had contacted him and wanted consulting work on the topic of successful investment strategies.

Evidently, this renowned firm had so biased its own research department to always present information in a sales manner that it wanted something better, perhaps, for its best clients. Or that was what I thought.

Anyway, it was the assignment of a lifetime. This was the key to money management, and money management was the key to Wall Street at the time.

Ken Beggs called me just as my own thinking had moved beyond the Institute. I had reached the conclusion that my future was with the securities industry. I too read the response of the investment-banking report as a signal for the future.

From my position, I felt that going to work as a securities analyst would be the best way for me to enter the field. And so I contacted the brokerage houses in San Francisco to see if there were openings as an analyst.

I was lucky.

Shuman Agnew, which was the white-shoe firm on the street, wanted to replace its banking and financial institutions analyst with someone else. Rich Kingsley was director of research, and I met with him, and we got along very well. He called my one reference on the street, Tony Barber, who was Jim Barker's roommate at Columbia, and Tony gave me a heads-up recommendation. Jim Barker was three years my junior in attending Columbia College. Tony also attended Columbia.

All of this showed that the old boy network was still at work. And it seemed so remote, but just a few friends are all that is needed to open doors. San Francisco is just about as far as you can get from New York City, but there it was.

At that late night meeting, I had to tell Ken Beggs what

I had done. He was disappointed, and I never heard what happened to that assignment. But I was soon to be launched as a securities analyst.

I often think of that point in my work. I was really destined to go into the securities business one way or another. Maybe the way the Institute would have provided would have been better. Once this assignment would have been completed, I would have been the leading expert in strategies of money management in the country and which ones worked well and which ones were less successful. And which ones should be avoided. There would be no way of telling where this could lead. In the end, I might have held any number of positions or had my own money management firm.

As it turned out, this is exactly what happened seven years later. As I look back, it was as if a big hand was pushing me in this direction, and it didn't matter which way I took to get there.

All of this was beyond my thinking at the time.

Closer to home, the Palo Alto days were filled with sounds of Sylvi and Alan, keeping the house in an uproar, running in and out of the house, playing games in the yard, going to swimming lessons, and putting on little plays for Maie and me.

The swimming lessons were very important as it turned out. Both Sylvi and Alan became champion swimmers. Alan won the prizes, but Sylvi was just as good as a swimmer. Alan had the strength, the power to carry him to the finish. It was a magnificent sight to behold when he raced. That was evident right from the start, as he was taking lessons. And how important it was for him to get started in this sport when he was young.

There were some incentives to all of this. The best one was to award him with a matchbox model car. He loved these miniature cars and would push them around the room endlessly.

At first, he didn't like to get his head under water. Then he became comfortable with this, especially after he saw that Sylvi did it. By the time he was four years old, he already showed the markings of a fine, champion swimmer.

Sylvi was always the graceful swimmer. With her, the motions through water appeared to be effortless. It was as if the water parted ways, and she just fitted into the opening. She quickly learned all of the well-known strokes and never seemed to be out of breath.

All of the lessons were held at the Ad Jaynes Swim Club, which I am grateful was still in business when the children needed the school. This swimming location was close to our home, just over a few streets on Willow Road in Menlo Park.

Then there were the wonderful birthday parties and the get-togethers of parents. And visits of the grandparents, who were still strong and pitched in to make the times festive whenever they were around.

All in all, these were happy days. I was happy that I could come home from the Institute for lunch and say hello to everybody. And see everyone without anything having to be special. Instead of spending hours on a commute or late dinners with clients, I was with the people who counted the most.

Perhaps the most distinguished award came to both Alan and Sylvi. That was the plaque at Chuck Taylor's summer camp that had top names carved in a wood for the best performer at the camp during a record period of many years. There, for the boys, was Alan's name. And for the girls was Sylvi's name. It was an inauspicious plank, and most people never noticed it. But it was a big award in my book. I wish that I had asked for it when the camp closed.

As I look back, this was the happiest time of all. Of course, each time can be the happiest if we make it so. But these two years were the very best.

Chapter 16
Shuman Agnew & Co.
1973 to 1975

I was now part of the securities business. I walked into the offices of the venerable firm of Shuman Agnew as a newly minted senior securities analyst, shook hands with Rich Kingsley, the director of research, and he showed me to my desk. My desk! I never thought that I would not have an office. It was one of those things, as an economist, that you take for granted. Well, there was no office for me. Right off the bat I was crushed. But I didn't let on. I kept my cool—during the office hours, that is.

Yet when I arrived home, I burst into tears and told Maie that I had made a big mistake. She gave me her calm counsel and told me to wait a few days and see how things went. She told me it might not be as bad as it appeared.

In fact, it wasn't. I adjusted to the desk within a week, and two weeks later, I realized that having a desk in the middle of a sea of desks is what you want in the securities business. You are then able to hear everything that is going on, without staff meetings or memos from on high.

By the end of the month, I had learned the main points of the firm's business. I didn't know the details, and these were important. But I knew broadly what was going on. That was more than I ever learned in my previous jobs. What wonderful knowledge this was.

There is a certain élan about the working floor of a brokerage house. This was true for Shuman Agnew, but also for all other firms or at least all that I visited, and I believe that I visited most of them. During good markets, which was most of the time, there was a spirit of optimism, uplift, and speculation about everything. It was a get-up-and-go attitude toward everything.

Dark thoughts have no place in this élan. One doesn't want to be branded as a pessimist or a naysayer. That doesn't give one any stature.

I believe that it is stature that people in investment houses ascribe toward. At Shuman Agnew, Park Dingwell was the man of stature. First of all, he was taller than everyone. All were tall, well over six feet and two inches, except for two men who were under six feet. Nobody took these short men very seriously.

Of course money is the primary driving force in the securities business. But after a certain point, money usually gives way to stature.

Stature also meant being able to explain everything that happened instantaneously. Park did this by implying that unrevealed sources had told him the real story a while ago.

There was always enough factual information in these explanations to make them believable, and customers lapped up the stories. And in the end, it didn't seem to make much difference, as long as a company's earnings held up.

The research department of Shuman Agnew tried to sort out the facts of a company from the active imaginations of the sales staff, so that investors could base their decisions of stocks that they might buy on objective information.

Nevertheless, there was no assurance that objective information would provide better investment results. But nobody figured out that this outcome could happen.

For example, sometimes imagination opens the door to the fulfillment of pent-up demand that sweeps an industry into prominence, and this happens without anyone anticipating that it could be so powerful. Cellular telephones are an example, and flat-screen television is another, to mention two products that have been spectacularly successful beyond most of the original objective analysis.

In any event, salesmen like to sell a growth story. And the salesmen of Shuman Agnew were where the power of the firm resided. On top of that, the president of the firm had been a salesman and continued to be the largest producer of sales among all of the sales staff.

Thus, Rich Kingsley was really working to shift the basis of power of the firm away from the usual sales to individual investors. He was building a department which sold securities to institutions who reward firms that provide the new type of factual data.

I felt allegiance to Rich. He hired me, and I worked for him. But I could see that Rich was on a collision course with the president. The cracks could be papered over as long as profits of the firm were high. But heaven help Rich Kingsley and his people if profits should decline for any length of time.

In the meantime, I was learning the ropes of a securities analyst, and I was working with customers and could hear their questions and see what made them sit up and take notice. This was the most valuable experience of all.

Jim Maletis helped more than anyone at that time or subsequently. He would review a meeting with a customer and point out ways I could do the job better. I listened carefully, because Jim was always right.

Jerry Down also gave me many valuable suggestions. Philip Smith and Irene Hoover were there to help too. John Debs showed me how lightning-fast thinking could be useful, and Jim Berdell showed the power of data when it is used in an overwhelming manner. The friendship of the latter two analysts has strengthened over the years, I am glad to see happen.

Rich had big plans for his institutional group. He wanted it to be the leading institutional house outside of the East Coast. As part of that plan, he wanted to provide the definitive research report on each of the companies that the firm followed.

And so it was my task to prepare the first of these, which would be on the Bank of America. It was also the last of this kind of report, as events turned out.

Anyway, my report was seventy-five pages in length and was a more thorough review of the bank that existed anywhere, including the large New York houses. It was an instant success. All institutional investors wanted a copy, and there was widespread interest in meetings on the subject. Jim Maletis, in particular, kept me busy on the road. Jim has been a close friend ever after, always with my highest respect for his work.

My reward was to be made a partner of the firm and a vice president. My share of the partnership was one sixteenth of 1 percent, which was more symbolic than financial, but it meant a lot to me and to Maie.

While I was off in my corner doing my tasks, much larger events were taking place. The stock market had reached a high at the beginning of 1973. Rich Kingsley had warned the firm that we would likely be in for a prolonged and deep downturn. Iver Lyche, the head of the firm, never liked what he called negative outlooks. He generally overlooked Rich's bear-market calls, but as conditions in the market worsened, he became contemptuous of Rich, as if Rich was causing the dismal market condition.

During these years, I continued to give lectures at the Rutgers School of Banking at Rutgers University, which is located in New Brunswick, New Jersey. They were on capital markets.

At this time, the diversion of teaching was heaven-sent. It was refreshing to not see the pacing up and down the walkway of the firm, the dour looks, and blow offs when something didn't go right for someone. The teaching was a form of escape, just when it was needed.

I didn't have anything to say at the banking school that was earthshaking. Nevertheless, I gathered that people liked what I had to say, because they would come back the following day.

Teaching is great experience. You learn what you teach as you teach. Of course, you know the material that you plan to teach before you stand up. But you only really know it when you stand before an audience and begin to explain it.

Among all businesses, none has the dramatic swings in mood as the securities firms. When the market is strong, the joy and happiness knows no bounds. On the other hand, no business is more in the dumps than securities firms when the market heads lower. I had just joined the firm when a difficult environment hit the firm, and Rich's forecast was about to come true, more vividly than even he had imagined.

In this tumult, Iver requested that I prepare a report on Crocker National Bank. I told Iver that the bank was not a sound recommendation. It turned out that Iver's good friend was the president, and Iver wanted the report as some sort of trophy to help him. I didn't think that this was a good idea and told Iver this. Iver didn't like to hear this.

The outcome was that I was told my days with the firm were over, and wouldn't it be nice if I went across the street to the Bank of America to be their monetary economist under Lee Prussia? The bank might have felt some sort of obligation to me, since I had written the first full-scale institutional report on its activities. I hesitated, I don't know why, but I did.

Then the bank offered me a second position, in the cashier's department. The pressure to accept was made clear, and I accepted.

In certain ways, I was disappointed at my first years on Wall Street. It seemed that everything didn't work out. The truth was that I was gaining a first-rate training in the ways of the street, and that experience would prove to be very useful in the future.

I didn't know this at the time. But it didn't matter. I just kept plugging away.

Still, I had passed the forty-year mark and felt I had worked for years but was little better off than many people who had arrived in business just a year earlier.

But that was only the job. There was much more to those years, thanks to my family.

Sylvi and Alan were growing up and becoming little people. They had now become companions as well as the children that they also were. It was wonderful to see them as pals. They were four and seven years old. How beautiful and transitory were those years.

It was a time to show, explain, joke, and teach. Every minute was precious. They grasped everything like a magnet and kept what they had just learned. I loved to kid them by explaining things backward—seeing their expressions of disbelief, and letting them figure things out the right way, and then telling me how dumb I was.

I have always believed this experience honed their thinking and made them the critical observers that they became. Maie would always observe with a look of wondering what was happening, but she knew.

About this time, we needed to replace our two-door skylark Buick. I wanted to get a sports car that was also a classic car. I couldn't afford an imported sports car, so I confined my look to the American-made production cars.

The first of these cars was a 1966 Oldsmobile Cutlass Supreme.

Then I bought a 1965 Buick Skylark. This was painted dark metallic blue. It was a smaller car than the Oldsmobile. It was also a beautiful car, and it was just right in shape and proportion.

Sylvi was developing her friends and getting around town on her bicycle. She was becoming quite independent. We would often see her alight her cycle, take off to places unknown, sure that she would arrive home safe and unscathed.

That was one to the advantages of living in a home-minded community such as Palo Alto. You didn't have to worry. Cars drove relatively slowly, and mothers everywhere looked out for the children as they passed by.

Our house lot runs 360 feet deep. It is well planted with shrubs and trees. In the back of the lot, behind bushes and trees, the previous owners had built a small shed which housed yard equipment and was also a doghouse. Maie's father, Isa, looked at this small building and had ideas about enlarging it.

Over the years, he gradually added to it, converting it into a small guest house with a living-dining-kitchen area, a bedroom, and a bathroom, with a large walk-in closet. It is a peaceful, completely comfortable refuge.

There were lots of great moments as the house was being built. One involved Sylvi and Isa and showed her spunk in a good-natured way.

While Isa was building the first phase of construction, Sylvi climbed up a ladder and started to walk on the roof. Isa was shocked and greatly concerned that she might fall from the roof. He shouted to her in a strong voice to get down immediately. Sylvi was taken aback but obeyed.

When she put her foot on the ground she said to Isa that she would be all right on the roof. Isa said in a gruff voice that she should stay off the ladder. A couple of minutes went by and Isa looked up. There on the roof was Sylvi. Isa said, "I told you to keep off the roof." Sylvi said, "You told me to stay off the ladder. I climbed the tree." Sure enough, there was a tree growing up to the roof, with a strong trunk. Both parties made their point, but Sylvi got hers in too.

Only after we celebrated our new little house did we think about getting a permit to build it. I now believe that a permit application would have been turned down. Actually, nobody paid any attention to the house. There were many tall trees, and we had a large lot, so the guest house disappeared into what looked like unending greenery.

As Alan grew up, it became clear that he had a special way

with animals, especially pets. He always looked for some time to look after Woody, our cockapoo, which is short for a cocker spaniel and poodle breed.

Woody and Alan had a special relationship. Woody would lie by Alan motionless for time on end. I truly feel that they communicated with each other.

I have long felt that people who are close to animals are the most perceptive people of all. Alan was surely one of those people.

For several years, Maie had talked about when the time would come when people who had left Estonia might go back. Maie's father wasn't sure that time would come in his lifetime. We inquired from the United States Department of State and sources close to happenings in Estonia and were warned to stay away.

The Soviet government kept lists of enemies of the state, and woe to the person caught behind the Iron Curtain who would be on these lists. It was all part of the secret police activities of Soviet countries. Estonia was one of these countries.

But by the early 1970s, the mass deportations of the earlier decades had ceased, and the country began to appear stabilized. So I inquired once more and received a more positive response. As long as the person had nothing to do with conditions in the war with Germany and was not known to be antagonistic in an open way against the Soviets, they would provide safe passage in and out of their country.

That was clearly a change in attitude. Maie didn't fit into

the vulnerable group. She was a child when the war was fought, and she was not outspoken.

Still, I needed some personal confirmation. So I called my old high school and Columbia College friend Jack Swanson, who was then chief of information in Europe for the Central Intelligence Agency. We talked on the phone, and I asked him what the risks would be. Jack said that there had been a change in policy for several years and that it would be safe. They would let Maie out. For some reason, I never asked about myself. I just felt being an American, born in America, gave me special privileges, which was not true, of course.

So in 1973, Maie and I set out for Estonia. The only way in was through Helsinki on a boat. When we landed, we were interviewed three times, once by the Estonian-controlled police, again by a Soviet army official, and finally by a fierce, severe NKVD officer. The latter gentleman was straight from the secret police.

They all scared me, especially the last one. All of this took place in what looked like a run-down warehouse with no windows and a door guarded by soldiers with machine guns.

We were told we could go. We walked through the door, by the machine guns and into the sunlight. There, standing in a circle, were a dozen of Maie's relatives.

There were, as best as I recall, Mare and her young son Andres, Malle, Arvo, Vaike, Peeter, Greatuncle Anton, and Anne. As we walked closer to them, they were apprehensive and reserved for a moment. But only for a moment, until our eyes reached each other. We drew closer.

Each person held a bouquet of flowers. Then there were tears in the eyes. Anne had survived Siberian slave camps, and here they saw remnants of their family that had escaped to freedom. Each hug meant "You will be free, someday." Many wouldn't let go. It was a transcending moment.

Flowers were all they possessed. That and their presence. They handed us the flowers each in turn and gave a little speech. It was embracing and formal. I had never seen anything quite like this. It must have been like this a half century earlier. I think that because everything that communism touched had the effect of freezing it in time. Communism proclaimed itself as the wave of the future. Actually, it was a frozen piece of ice, locking people in an earlier age.

But the goodwill was overwhelming. Our visit continued to farms, homes, all sorts of walks—only then, in the forest or wide-open space, could you talk freely. Our hotel room had microphones. We knew we were being constantly watched.

Arvo Reial was a high-ranking official in the agricultural department, which was the main export of the country, and he had a state-provided car and chauffeur. So we traveled around in his car.

We were not supposed to go beyond military check points in Tallinn, but his position meant that we could travel with him to the interior of Estonia to the ancient university city of Tartu. There and everywhere, we were treated to the best food they could find and, to me, appeared to be enormous feasts. We felt like we were royalty visiting faraway lands with well-wishers that astounded belief.

How was this possible? Why did these people show so much warmth? Our empathy came nowhere near their joy at seeing us.

I think we represented hope. Hope that better could come. Hope that all had not been lost. Hope that this dastardly communist system would someday fall apart. Hope that a new birth of freedom would give rise to an outpouring of talents that now had no place to go and not a chance of development. It was power that would strengthen and prove to be more potent than all of the secret police lined up with submachine guns.

But that was for the future. For now, there was only hope in the mind, and we represented the living embodiment of this hope. That is what made our presence so emphatic.

The conditions of the place showed considerable deterioration. All buildings needed repair and paint. I couldn't believe that such a simple thing as paint would be in such short supply. But it was. Everything was gray and drab. Buildings were the same color as the streets. Every piece of clothing was precious.

There were some light moments. Our hotel was the Viru, and it was built by the Finns, because they could provide elevators that would reach fifteen floors. The rooms were small, and the mattresses were stiff and hard. Several rooms down from our room, there was a party going on. We tried to sleep, but the party kept getting louder.

Finally, we had to do something. So I went to the buxom lady that guarded the elevator door on our floor to complain about the commotion. She marched to the room, opened the door, turned off the radio, and then marched away. The brutal directness stunned everybody, and the party was over. At first we were motionless, then we laughed.

What an amazing trip. How wonderful it was to return home.

Chapter 17
Bank of America
1975 to 1981

I walked into the huge skyscraper that was the headquarters of the Bank of America, feeling like a crushed man once again. My children were growing up, and I was still close to an entry-level position. I felt this keenly at the bank with the group I was assigned to.

This was a group of nine bright young men who had a special task of figuring out how the bank could organize its books so that it could identify quickly where it was making money. It was a group that was part of the cashier's division, which is what banks call their treasurer's department.

I was soon to learn that nobody in the bank took them seriously. It was the brainchild of Lee Prussia, nevertheless; and since he was vice chairman, there was a certain tone of respect given to the group.

The group was headed by Mack Terry, one of the nicest people I have ever met. And Mack was completely dedicated to the bank, so much so that the hours away from his home, I believe, cost him his marriage. That was not a happy sight to see. But Mack was always a gentleman to everyone, including me.

For over a month, Mack didn't know what to do with me. I felt totally useless and wondered how long things would last here.

Then from on high came a request for me to prepare a presentation on the bank's competitive situation. This involved a comparison of the basic financial and market measures. I was given the assignment, and it was right up my road. I knew how to do this blindfolded.

Lee Prussia, who was also the bank's junior chief financial officer, was to introduce me. Lee had made the offer for me to join the bank. Lee was always pleasant to me, but I never felt that I was on his team.

Within a few weeks, I was ready, and I gave the report to the managers of the world banking group. It went over very well, and I was asked to present it to the bank's managing committee. Clarence Baumhefner sat on this group. He was the bank's chief financial officer, and he asked a number of questions. He never said anything, ever, that reflected anything positive to anybody.

Then for some reason I never heard about, I was asked to give the talk before the bank's board of directors. This simply didn't happen to new employees working with entry-level people. Anyway, the talk went very well. I returned to my desk and was assigned a task with the group's ongoing work of developing this new accounting system that Mack Terry was all wrapped up with. I was told by one of the old hands of the bank, Art Holter, that I should keep my head down and work at this profitability project, or I would be sidetracked to nothing worthwhile. This was as frank as you could get. I had been with the bank for a year, and this is what my task would be. I had never been in such a place and could see why people had nervous breakdowns. I still had a chance to find someplace else, but many people at the bank didn't have this choice.

I didn't fit in at all. But I put my shoulder to the wheel. I looked ahead to a nine-to-five job until I would be sixty-five years old and then retire. There was nothing on the horizon that I could see.

Yet behind the scenes, my talk had set off a controversy in the bank. It showed that the bank would no longer be the largest bank in the world unless it dramatically stepped up its deposit-gathering capability. It showed how this weakness would give First National Bank of New York the advantage within three to four years. This hit a matter of pride to the senior bank people, who felt that being the biggest bank in the world was a heritage that they had been entrusted with.

So I got a call from the bank's chief economist, Walter Hoadley, who also happened to be on the board. And that was nice. But still I kept my head down and worked on this seemingly unending project of accounting for bank profits. Despite my personal frustration, I could see the great value the results of the task could show. It would simply tell the bank's management where it was making money and where it was not. At the time, this was only a reasoned guess.

About this time, I felt that my suits didn't really fit right. I was surrounded by people whose clothing really fit. And it became clear, looking around the bank, that suits were really a uniform. Depending on the material and fit, your suit said you were a corporal or a colonel or even a general. Of course, this was all so subtle to the untrained eye. But in the top banking and corporate world, it was obvious to the one who looked.

I certainly didn't want to look like a corporal in that environment. So I put aside some money and went to the respected clothier Brooks Brothers, went to the second floor, and asked for a banker's gray hand-tailored suit. That opened the door to Chris, who was my consultant and advisor, and fittings and all of the rest. Chris knew how to do everything right. I won't tell how much this cost. But it was worth it. I did look different. I would say the suit said "colonel" and that was good enough.

Ever after, I have always wanted a few pieces of clothing, but the best. And I never look at bargains as the first cut. I really believe you have to look right to be fully accepted in whatever circumstances you find yourself.

While all of this was going on, Sylvi and Alan were growing up. And they were growing up as nice young people. A large part of this was due to Maie's steady hand at the wheel in training them properly. She did all of the hard work in training.

She knew what needed to be done. I was not skilled in this as she was. What wonderful luck that she had this talent.

Both Sylvi and Alan joined up with soccer teams in the local area which was part of the American Youth Soccer Organization. This organization was entirely sponsored by parents, who acted as coaches for the teams. That gave it a closeness that was never possible with school-sponsored sports.

I also became coach of a team that Alan was on, after I left the bank, and had the free time in the afternoon to give to the team and organization. But while I was with the bank, the most that I could do was watch the soccer matches from the sidelines.

In addition to soccer, Sylvi and Alan were on baseball teams. Sylvi was on a girls' softball team, and Alan was on a little league team.

Maie and I would go dutifully to all of these games. They were often in the windswept afternoons in the springtime, when the winds would chill every bone. But we would stand bravely, as we regarded it to be our duty to cheer the team on to whatever the outcome happened to be.

Alan's teachers worked hard with him, wanting to bring out what talents that they knew were inside him. One teacher, Mrs. Schoenberger, had a meeting with us and actually began to cry, as she thought about him. She said that she felt he was one of the most talented students she had ever taught, but this talent was not forthcoming very easily.

I always walked away from these kinds of meetings more befuddled than informed. Of course, that was not the purpose of the meeting.

I don't think I was a good father during this period. I had become wrapped up in work, just to find my way. I was approaching fifty years, and that was a watershed point in my thinking.

And then there were Sylvi and Alan. I wasn't doing all that I should to be with Sylvi and Alan and to help them or at least to be there in their room every day, just to be near them. And I should be looking about the scene in Palo Alto and San Francisco to see what was going on that they would be interested in seeing.

I sometimes thought that it would be nice to follow the career paths that had become so embedded in corporate life, where one step led to another. But I never realized at the time that for every step up, there were three sideways steps by other people.

I was too much wrapped up in myself. I didn't realize this at the time.

As a special treat, I took everybody, including Maie's parents, to Grand Cayman. We rented a small beach house that was twenty steps to the water. Maie's father remembered this vacation as the best in his experience. He loved the warm and almost-still water. All of us wanted to stay forever in the little beach house. Someday, we will have to go back.

One of the interesting people I met at this time was Kevin

Boden, who was running a radio talk show. He invited me to be a guest on his show, and we struck up a friendship that continued on after that. It was first-rate experience to go on a talk show, and Kevin showed me all of the ropes, so that when I went on TV shows in New York and Tokyo, I was as cool as a cucumber.

As I think of Kevin, I am reminded at how fortunate I have been to meet people who become personal friends.

Kevin and his wife, Maria, were close to our family for another reason. Both of our families had lost their son. In the case of Kevin and Maria, it was a fire that engulfed their home. Workmen had finished applying floor treatment, which ignited when their son was in the house to look at the work that had been done that day, and waiting for the parents to come home.

Kevin and Maria will always be close to us.

Everything held together because Maie was there for all of us. She kept the home fires burning, and they burned brightly, thanks to her steady efforts to make life a positive experience for all of us.

Then one day, out of the blue, a fairly short, but very polite and pleasant man came by my desk at the bank and said he was Jim Robinson and that I would be working for him. It was so casual and so considerate—he came by to see me—that I was taken off my feet. I hadn't the slightest idea of what he did.

He took me to the second floor and showed me my new desk. Now the second floor was really three floors of ceiling space, all done in granite with deep burgundy area carpets. It was a class-act floor. And there were no offices. It was a place where, as they say in banking, you walked the walk and talked the talk. In short, it was a showplace, and you quickly showed whether you might fit into elegant surroundings.

I was sorry to leave the old quarters. I had made many good friends, including Ray Gordon, who would play an important role in the development of Bank Valuation, and Dave Coulter, who sat two desks away from me.

Dave would soon be made president of the bank. But as events showed, and I predicted, he was not prepared to take on this job and perform successfully. He had never worked with customers nor had he ever made a loan, which is the essential business of a bank. His sale of the bank was one of the major mistakes of American business of the period.

I then learned that I had been transferred to the world banking division. This was the elite division of the bank, where everyone had advanced degrees in business or something, and everyone had attended one of the eleven best universities as identified by Tom Clausen, the president of the bank. This was elitism carried further than I had ever seen. The fact is that it is common in most major financial institutions.

At first, I didn't know quite what to make of Jim. He was the least likely person to be a top-scale person. Of course, he was the most pleasant of men in the bank. But he didn't look the part. He looked a little frumpy. I sat at my desk wondering what in the world was happening. I figured it had to be good, because I was sitting in the gilded cage of the bank. And Jim must have something going for him to be here too.

It turned out that Jim was doing much of what Mack Terry was doing, but Jim did it on a higher level; his conclusions were much briefer, and although I didn't think it could be possible, he was a lot smarter than Mack.

He would call on me maybe once or twice a week. I would produce what he asked for in a few hours and then would look as if I were doing something important as customers would walk by and surveyed the place. Soon I felt bold enough to work on the book which I had decided to write.

The book had a grand design to give the reader the tools necessary to evaluate a bank from all business perspectives. It would be called *Bank Analyst's Handbook*. I started to spread papers out on my desk and was reminded that a neat desk is looked upon with favor. Jim didn't pay much attention to the book, and from that point on, I kept it mostly under wraps. But I was making progress, and that made me happy.

Jim and I became good friends, and our friendship grew as time went on. I didn't do much for him, but he seemed to be effusive in his compliments. I could only guess that he must have had terrible help before. Maie and I also became good friends with his wife, Terry, and his son and two daughters, one of whom he lost due to a heart condition. Our family shared his family's sadness when this happened.

I began to get requests for special projects from Al Rice, who was vice chairman of the bank. I was selected, I began to realize, because of my experience in the cashier's division. All of that work with Mack Terry was now useful. All of this innocence began to give way when Al Rice began to ask for what might, in some quarters, be considered to be confidential information. I really didn't know how to handle this. One thing was for sure. I didn't want to get what could be described as someone with an insider reputation.

Then came the announcement that Al Rice had resigned, as the phrase goes. Actually he appears to have been fired. I dimly recall that it had something to do with Robert Vesco, a notorious fugitive from the Federal Bureau of Investigation. So that settled that problem.

Then one day, I answered the phone, and Chauncey Medberry's secretary was on the line and asked if I were free. This was the chairman of the bank. I told her that I was free, and hopped on an elevator to the fortieth floor. I arrived at his office, only to find that he wasn't there. His secretary apologized and suggested that I wait for him and wouldn't I like to sit in his chair behind his desk.

I walked over to his desk and knew that was not the place for me. Nobody but Chauncy Medberry should sit at that desk. I sat in another chair for a half of an hour and then left. I never understood all of that but now believe that I should have waited all night, if necessary, for him to return. I am sure that this was some sort of test. The bank was full of these things, especially if you were being reviewed for something.

One day, Jim said I was to go to the Philippines for a seminar for Asian world bank division executives. He set the trip up so that I could spend the weekend in Hong Kong. I did my duty to explain Mack Terry's building block system and then went on to Hong Kong.

That city changed my life in thinking about the best way to develop a country's economy. Instead of aid to a monopolistic government, they set up a currency board to ensure the integrity of their currency and promoted open-market competition. The wealth literally flowed into the streets. I had never seen such abundance. When I got home, at the runway in the airport, I said to Maie that we should get on the next plane and go there. It was beyond my fondest dreams.

Then there was another change. I was to be put under a young banker, who got his position, I heard from several people, in part because his father had been president of the Federal Reserve Bank of Chicago. A good family, as the saying goes in banking, still counts for a lot. He was a hard-charging ex-marine. I found his directness to be refreshing. I got along with him very well. We both liked to laugh at the same jokes.

Jim Robinson died several years after we worked together. He had left the bank after moving to New York, and he was working for the European Central Bank, sorting things out in Budapest. One of the regrets of my life is that I did not attend his funeral. Now I would have done so in a moment's notice. I think that highly of him.

Then came the call from Joe Chiappetta. That was the call that changed my career in a big way. But there are some other things to look at before we see into that.

Chapter 18
Ventures
1977 to 2011

I had tried my hand in banking, securities markets, and corporate planning. Somehow, I felt let down, and I didn't know what was wrong. I was in my fifties, and I felt that I was still at the bottom of the barrel.

I talked with a few close friends, older gentlemen who might have some experience to share. One wonderful friend, also a Columbia College old timer, Siggy Kempner, was always a welcome ear. But his solution was only temporary. He would open his bottom drawer and pull out a pint of good scotch, share a couple of drinks, and take me to lunch at the Stock Exchange Club, which was a delightful place. But I needed something better.

All of this was driven home one evening after a talk by Professor Henry Graf, who was my principal advisor at Columbia College. He came to San Francisco to get more enthusiasm among the alumni. After his talk, I joined a circle of friends that surrounded him. I had not seen him for more than twenty years, so I introduced myself. That wasn't necessary. He recognized me at once and was genuinely interested in seeing me again.

He asked me what I was doing, and I told him that I worked for the Bank of America. He then asked me, with a twinkle in his eye, what kind of vice president I might be. Of course I was not any kind of vice president, so I said something evasive. The good professor noticed this immediately, then someone distracted him, and I mercifully escaped.

Driving home that evening with Maie, I went over the scene in my mind, and I decided that I would expand my activities in the hope that something better would emerge.

On that drive home, I resolved that I would write the most basic book on banking. Nobody at the bank had written even a single book on banking. No one would be able to overlook this book.

After a few days of thinking about a title, I settled on writing on how one could analyze and value a bank. Nothing could be simpler nor more basic.

Bank Analyst's Handbook

This book was to turn out to be the first of ten ventures that I would pursue over the next three decades. All were in addition to my regular jobs.

The book was to be a practical book. It was for people working in the field who were called on to make decisions virtually at a moment's notice.

These people want to grasp the essentials that go into decisions.

Of course, banks are complicated businesses. When they are analyzed for book value—that is how much they would be worth if they would be sold to bidders in an open market—the issues become elaborate and complex. The handbook recognizes this and shows that you can still make good decisions without that and other complex refinements.

It shows how different users of a bank need to focus their thinking and which information is important to emphasize.

The book sold nearly seven thousand copies at a final price of $89.95 each, and it was considered to be a success by John Wiley & Sons, the publisher.

The publisher asked me to revise the book. I declined because I had other commitments, and its purpose, which was to get a promotion within the bank to vice president, was accomplished. What a great day that was.

The effects of the book carried on beyond the bank. In fact, the book was widely used in graduate business schools, and at the Stanford Business School, it was kept within the business school library, which is reserved for the most important books of the curriculum

The book was also the basis of Bank Valuation, which will be discussed shortly.

The Money Analyst

This report provided an outlook for financial markets, with an emphasis on how money supply affects these markets.

The broader role of the central bank was also given attention. The impact of the central bank on quality rankings was also discussed. The report forecast interest rates two years into the future.

The report was intended for use by money managers and portfolio managers, as well as individual investors who managed their own money.

The report added two dimensions that were not usually found in conventional forecasts of interest rates. First, it looked at the important long-term cycles that pervade all bond yields. Second, it adjusted interest rates for inflation, which provided a measure of real interest rates. These are the rates that people really use on a day-to-day basis.

I sold this report as a monthly subscription, two hundred sixty-five dollars per year with twelve issues.

My peak sales amounted to 170 subscriptions.

The report was intended to be a standalone venture. But in an unexpected development, it served as my entry into Jefferies & Co., Inc., as will be discussed later. This was a very favorable development, and I felt it had far more potential than as a standalone monthly newsletter. Jefferies could provide a large platform. In fact, the platform would turn out to be larger than I could imagine. For this reason, I discontinued selling subscriptions. The *Money Analyst* lived on, but with the Jefferies name on its cover.

Nevertheless, if Jefferies had not come along, the report could have been the basis for opening a money-management company. But that prospect would have been well into the future.

Either way, the report was a valuable property, which could have taken several directions. But it is a good thing to have too many opportunities. It is not a good thing to have too few.

Timing

This was a personal finance book that discusses how you can best use your money during each of the seven stages that exist in a person's life cycle. These stages of the life cycle are described by Eric Erickson over the course of his career as a psychologist. Many psychologists believe that he was the most important psychologist in the twentieth century.

The book was published by Argus Communications, Inc. It was not successful, largely because it was never aggressively marketed. The book had some avid followers, but at the time, there was no way for these people to meet one another and share their enthusiasm. That would have built a strong base to expand sales. There have been enormous changes in book selling over the past twenty-five years, and if the book were to be launched today, the results probably would have been stronger.

Power and Wealth: How Presidents Cause Stock Market Rallies and Crashes

The third book that I wrote was the story about the powerful connection between the chairman of the central bank and the president. The socially polite way of expressing this is to say that the two are independent and go their separate ways to govern the country.

The book points out that this is nothing like what goes on. The reality is that the president, in almost every case, had used the central bank to his advantage.

But there have been instances where the central bank has revolted. Usually, this occurs when the bond houses in New York believe that the president would be taking a ruinous course.

The book concludes by showing how the central bank exerts its power through money-supply flows and the Treasury exerts its power through tax rates. The combination of these forces largely sets the course for stock prices.

It was published by Menlo Publishers and sold for $13.95. Again, a lack of promotion caused the book to be little read by the general public. But among my clients throughout the world, it was widely read and commented on.

The book would have been an excellent reference piece to launch an investment-management company. It was just waiting to happen. But once again, I had a full plate with other things.

Then Maie and I participated in two investment companies.

The companies were formed with Derek Anderson and his wife, Pat. I was a director of both companies. The first was

CD Anderson & Co., Inc.

and the second was

Anderson Capital Management, Inc.

The first company was a discount stock-trading firm. This company prospered and, at one time, was one of the principal discount-trading houses on the West Coast.

This stock-trading firm was ripe for picking, and Security Pacific National Bank, which was then the second largest bank in the West, made a highly advantageous offer to acquire the operation. It was carried through, and the proceeds covered Alan's college expenses from beginning to end.

Naturally, I expected the second company to do as well. The asset management company was off to a good start, and after a year and a half of working with customers, the firm had acquired twenty-six million dollars in assets under management.

This was a good base to build upon. At this point, Derek felt that the firm needed more capital, and all of us put up more cash.

Then quite unexpectedly, Derek decided to close the business. I was shocked. But what could I do. Derek had run the firm and was not interested in having another person come into the role of managing director. He and Pat were the majority shareholders, so their wishes would be followed.

I told Derek this would be a terrible loss and produced numbers. But Derek took a deaf ear to my protestations—and pleas.

The situation left me sad.

Stickney & Herrick, Inc.

This was a copy shop which grew out of producing the *Money Analyst*. It flourished for three years, then competition from new types of printing and the discovery that money was being stolen by the manager to satisfy drug addiction, caused it to be closed down. The personal loss was minimal, because I had earlier sold the company to new owners.

Bank Valuation, Inc.

This company almost made it. It was the most promising of all the start-ups. In addition to myself, there were two other partners. Neil Reilly was the account representative. I had met him at Jefferies & Co. In fact, Neil came to me with the idea of starting this company. Ray Gordon, the other member of the team, had been part of Mack Terry's group at the Bank of America. I had also been part of this group at one point.

Neil was the salesman, Ray was the computer man, and I was the idea man. We were to share equally in the profits.

The name of the company told what it was. The company showed which banks were least at risk and those most at risk. Banks ranked low were considered to have a higher risk of default, and thus, they should be expected to pay more for their funds. By the same token, banks which were soundest would be expected to pay less. There were, of course, many ways this principle applied in pricing of funds and services of banks.

The main advantage of this company was that there was no

conflict of interest in what it did. This was not the case with its competition, including Moody's and Standard and Poor's. These latter companies were paid by the companies that they were valuing, not by the customers who needed this information to be accurate and uncompromised.

Our company would be paid by the people who used the information. That was the ethical way of doing business.

We had fifteen customers at five thousand dollars per customer, and then the stock market collapsed in 1987. Neil could no longer work for a small retainer. The main source of our income was from a law firm that retained us for a law suit that was unrelated to Bank Valuation.

That meant that without outside capital, the company would have to fold. We were one year from the break-even point. Looking back, we should have gone to a venture capitalist to see if anything could be done. That was my fault due to lack of foresight.

As matters turned out, by the late 1990s, this firm would have been the only independent bank-valuation service in the world. It might have been worth a lot of money by 2010.

Avalon Capital Management

This money-management firm has been in business for more than a decade and has prospered nicely and gradually. Maie and I are minority founding investors. We own less than 10 percent of the company.

The company has gradually increased its payout and is a long-term investment which we have not disturbed.

The company is headed up by Dave Rahn, who is one of the best investment managers in the business.

Someday, when the stock market gets really hot again, which it will, this firm will be sought by banks and insurance companies. It could be worth a sizeable sum.

The Private Bank of the Peninsula

One day, a good friend, Bill Phillips, and I had lunch together. Bill and I are members of the Palo Alto Club and frequently see each other at the club. Bill was driving, and on the way back to my house, he said that he and some friends were organizing a new bank in Palo Alto and asked if I would be interested to participate. I was enthusiastic about the prospect. I became the largest individual investor on the board of directors.

The bank would lend to the Palo Alto area and would focus on profitability, rather than growth of assets. That was exactly what I wanted.

Jim Wall, whom I knew, would be chairman. He is a superb banker.

Everything looked perfect. I tried to think of what could go wrong, but nothing important came to mind. I reviewed the investment with three business-savvy friends, and they could find nothing amiss either.

The stock came to market at the equivalent of ten dollars per share, after adjustment for a ten to one distribution. The stock rose to seventeen dollars per share. Everything was like a rose garden.

During the first year, the bank grew slowly. This didn't

bother me. It had solid loans, and the bank was building on solid ground.

But two of the directors on the board grew dissatisfied with slow growth in the next year. They wanted growth at all costs. This meant aggressive marketing and loans that could eventually prove to be risky and some could fail. The bank would be reaching for what I saw could eventually backfire.

I saw a stormy future ahead, especially since this insurgent group of directors was beginning to prevail. I could not agree with this direction, so I resigned from the board.

In two years from my departure, loans did run into difficulty. The bank's stock price fell to one-half of its price at the initial public offering.

Subsequently, the bank has righted itself. Now the bank is on its way to do what I originally felt it should do.

So here over a thirty-year period were ten ventures that were outside my regular daily work. Two were very successful, two were failures, and six were so-so. For venture companies, that is not a bad record. Most venture firms are happy with less.

Three messages emerge from this lifetime of ventures. First, if the work involves writing, is in my hands, and is marketed, it will probably be successful. Second, there must be a personal commitment of time on my part. I must be on deck leading the troops. Third, I must speak about what it means to people.

I have taken these messages to heart. They point to more books and fewer businesses. There is nothing as powerful as a mind which has been awakened.

Chapter 19
Pine Mountain Lake
1972 to Present

We first visited Pine Mountain Lake when Alan was still in diapers. We planted him in the sand, looking out to the water, and he waddled like a duck into the water, never looking back. It was sunset, and the sight of this infant in the wide realm of nature is one of the most beautiful memories I have of Alan.

Over the years, Pine Mountain Lake became our refuge. It actually is a real estate development, which was set up and financed by Boise Cascade. It was so well designed and is so beautiful in such a magnificent setting that even subsequent heavy-handed developers couldn't ruin it.

The development is at an elevation of three thousand feet, so it is always accessible in the winter. And in the summer, its temperature is warm, sometimes hot.

I first learned of the place in a newspaper advertisement. For our first visit, we rented a basement of a house, and from that point forward, this place was always our favorite vacation location.

The center of the development is a large lake. There is a swimming pool; there are tennis courts, stables for horses, sail boats and paddle boats, movie nights under the starry sky—everything kids who love to be out of doors would cherish. There is also a jet airport.

Many of our happiest moments were here. We were always busy with some race or some activity. It was not a place where worries flourished about some business or school matter. Life was good here, and we didn't let anything get in the way of this attitude.

It was at Pine Mountain Lake that Alan and Sylvi perfected their swimming styles. This was several years before they entered competitive swimming in high school. The coaching they received here also occurred before they both won the all-round-athlete award at the Chuck Taylor summer camp program.

Pine Mountain Lake was also the place where Sylvi and Alan could explore their abilities in a quiet way.

Sometimes this was not what we had in mind.

For example, Alan had just finished learning the overhand stroke, and with that, he added new knowledge to his already-considerable strength. He found his swimming range was literally extended as far ahead as he could see. He wanted to test that new skill and his already-evident power.

So he and Sylvi planned to swim across the lake. You were not supposed to do this. The swimming area was a small roped-off section of the main beach.

Sylvi would swim on a life preserver, which would be ready for Alan if he should need it. They swam beyond the rope boundary of the swimming area and headed to open water. Well over half way to the opposite shore, someone discovered what had happened and called the lake patrol, which had a high-speed boat. Once alerted, this boat sighted the swimmers and took off at top speed.

The patrol men pulled Alan and Sylvi out of the water and took them back to the swimming area, also at top speed, admonishing them along the way. Alan loved the boat ride and often talked about it afterward. There certainly was excitement. Maie and I, of course, knew nothing at all about this. We learned of it months later.

At Pine Mountain Lake, everything happens slowly. Everything is personal. Nobody could fail. Everybody only succeeds, but at various paces. It was like America in the dreams of a bygone era, before the various movements we see and hear around us.

Sylvi and Alan would bring their friends. When they were old enough to drive, we would often have a houseful of young people sleeping on beds, sofas, and on the floor. Before night and sleep overtook them, they would sit on the beach, hear the small waves, and talk into the deep night, telling each other their hopes and dreams, while Maie and I had long before closed our eyes for the evening.

Everyone was perfectly safe. There were guards at the gate, but nobody paid much attention to them. Yet they were there.

In 1980, I had made nearly seventy thousand dollars from three years of royalties from *Bank Analyst's Handbook*. I had asked the publisher, John Wiley & Sons, to accumulate these payments and to keep them as deferred royalties. They were very happy to do this and earn interest for themselves on the total. I didn't worry that they held this cash. Rather, I wanted the sum to be there when I wanted it. I didn't want this money to be frittered away on little things.

Then Maie chose a lot, and we bought it for seven thousand dollars. We were ready to build our vacation home.

I had spoken to an electrician who was working on a nearby house, Darrell Scott, and was impressed by his knowledge of general building. He had built his own house, but not one for someone else.

Most of all, I felt he was reliable from the way he talked. So I decided to ask him for an estimate. His number for the complete house was almost precisely the amount that was in the deferred royalties account at Wiley.

All of this sounds risky. There are many stories of builders who go broke and leave big problems for the prospective home owner. I only used my judgment of Darrell's character, and it turned out that I was right. Darrell was completely reliable and honest.

I have always felt that I could judge character. I don't know how I do this.

For example, one day, one of Maie's partners, a doctor, came to our door and asked me to give her a box with something in it from the medical laboratory. When I looked at him, I instantly felt a sense of grave danger. I politely took the box and shut the door.

Maie was upset and told me I was rude and that I should have invited him into our home. I told Maie that he was an evil person and that he must never see her or our children—ever.

Later, this doctor was terminated from his medical job for rumored bad and improper activities.

Then there is the other side. When Maie and I were looking for a nanny for Alan, when he was still very young, we had a parade of people in our home helping with Alan. One day, a lady by the name of Ruth Albin came to the door. I showed her Alan's room and asked her to sit down.

I went to the kitchen where Maie was preparing dinner and whispered into her ear that we now had found exactly the right person. I told Maie we should hire her right here and now. Ruth proved to be the most reliable and loving nanny whom we could ever have hoped for. And Alan grew to love her as his very special person. She truly was sent to us.

One of the loveliest weddings Maie and I have attended was the one for Desiree Dodson, daughter of Craig and Shelly Dodson. Those two also have a daughter, Amber.

This is the part of the family which descended from my uncle Avery, who was my grandfather's brother, who died untimely from carbon monoxide in the late nineteen thirties.

He left his wife, Hulda, and three children, Dave, Pat, and Joyce.

Pat was a booster all her life. She always saw the best in everyone, and she was a joy to have in your company.

Dave was more severe in his presence. I always liked him, and he treated me well, but he felt my grandfather had not been helpful to him after the death of his father. I never knew this until recently.

Joyce is the person you always want to have beside you. She knows how to help get things done and never be in the way. She is always cheerful, and that counts for a lot when the going gets rough.

One day, I was going through some old family pictures and found a remarkable photograph of a striking gentleman with sharp features and who looked like a prominent public figure. I asked my dad who this was. He said the picture was that of Avery, and it was likely taken right after he had died, which was a custom in those days.

I wanted to know more. I couldn't imagine such a vigorous man could have died from anything ordinary. After telling me about the garage door being shut and the engine of his car being turned on, he said that Avery liked to gamble at private men's clubs in Cleveland, as well as elsewhere. According to my dad, these clubs were run by gangsters, even though they appeared to be respectable. The hardened criminal element called all of the final shots.

My dad said that Uncle Avery had gambled too much and then doubled up, making a debt that would be impossible ever to pay. The criminal element then came to him and said they needed payment immediately, or the safety of his children could not be assured.

Uncle Avery then went to my grandfather, who was the older brother by two years, and pleaded for at least some funds.

All of this took place against a background of a second, more severe downturn of the business depression. Homes were being abandoned, cars were being offered at ridiculously low prices, and those that still had jobs faced a new round of firings. It was the darkest hour of the Depression.

My dad said that my grandfather was shaken to the bone. He did not have any money except his monthly paycheck, which came in the form of a deposit to his checking account. The amount that Uncle Avery needed was way above that, and it was above the value of my grandparents' home. The home was mortgaged. My grandfather was even paying on debts from the 1929 stock market crash. In fact, he even owed debts from this period when he died thirty years later. One was from something called the Mapes estate, where he paid fifty dollars a month until the day he breathed his last. My father paid it off.

Uncle Avery tried but could find no help. My father said that he probably took his own life. His insurance would apply to the debt.

My father said that my grandfather helped the family when the insurance company balked at payment, claiming that the death was not accidental. He hired two physicians to perform an autopsy, and he himself witnessed the event. He arranged for the best legal counsel to force the insurance company to pay the family. The insurance company did pay.

Pat and her husband, Proctor, had four children: George, who married sparkling Francoise from France, Craig, who married Shelly, who is a master pianist, Laurie, who married Carl, whose mind is as brilliant as you can find, and Averill, whose letters keep us informed and spread warmth and good cheer.

What a wonderful family to be a part of. I do have one small hope, and that is that members of our family might consider passing this memoir along to their families, so that it might live on for many more to see and read and touch, as I have touched it.

As I think about my branch of the family and the Dodson branch, it seems to me that we should be closer.

Pat worked for this when she was active. When we spoke, she always gave me an update on what everyone was doing. I liked that a lot. Now Craig tunes me in with his computer, which keeps us linked. I like that a lot too.

I am so impressed with the good moments we have when we are together; we should not let the opportunities for these moments slip by.

After Alan died and Sylvi moved away, our home at Pine Mountain Lake was used very little. Yet every time we go there we feel its charm and magic once again.

We let other friends and their family use it. Hartwell Brown, our computer aide, and his wife, Anna, used it for their honeymoon, and Marie Weninger, our house lady, took her family there a number of times.

We arranged for the gardening men at the lake to plant a tree in the marina, which is the beach that everybody eventually goes to visit. The tree is a plane tree, much like the sycamore back in Ohio. That was fifteen years ago.

In the years that have passed, this tree has grown tall and sturdy. It now shades large areas of grass, and it is a favorite spot for picnics and lounging in the open air.

There is a plaque identifying Alan as a swimmer and filmmaker. The plaque is made from bronze and will last a long time.

We have thought of selling our home at Pine Mountain Lake. Recently, we contacted a real estate agent about this. The agent told us that it would bring only a small sum and that the current market was unfavorable.

I was really delighted to hear this. I told Maie how wonderful it is that the property is too cheap to sell. We'll just have to keep it.

Chapter 20

Travel

1977 to 1995

All of us love to travel. A trip together always gave us moments of good companionship. That made me happy—we had each other.

The feeling of good cheer extended to all who also came along—Sylvi's boyfriend, and later her husband, Matthias Herzog, and Alan's girlfriend, Tracy Kinney—all were part of our traveling troupe.

These trips were some of the happiest moments of my life. Our family became an island. We were together, and the rest of the world was way far away.

It started out very modestly. We didn't realize what travel meant to us.

Ever since we were married, we traveled to visit Maie's parents in Winnipeg, usually once a year. They were pleasant visits. Often, Sylvi and Alan would visit their grandparents on their own.

Maie's father took great pleasure in showing Alan how to fish and how to clean a fish and finally how to cook a fish in the wilderness.

The two of them would go camping and what an education about nature Maie's father would give Alan. Just to be in his company in the woods was an education.

Nobody thanked Maie's father for this wonderful gift. It seems too late to do this now, but it must be done. He took Alan under his wing, and Alan came out stronger and a deeper person.

Similarly, Sylvi learned sewing and cooking from Maie's mother on those visits. She took patience to show Sylvi just what to do in the kitchen and on the dinner table. She too was an unsung hero in my estimation.

One day, Maie's father started to build a tree house on land that they had bought in the country. Sylvi and Alan hoisted their meals up to a perch and sat high above the ground while they enjoyed lunch.

So our travel began within the close family. We kept this family touch as we extended the scope of the travel. And on one occasion, we went halfway around the world with everybody on board.

Our first trip as a foursome family, Maie, Sylvi, Alan, and myself, was to Disneyland in Southern California. Tom and Judy Bowen and their family joined us. This was a remarkably joyous time. We all clicked together. It was also the first of many get-togethers.

Next was Vancouver, British Columbia. We drove on this

trip, and we stopped for a few days at Sun River, Oregon, which is a resort for families. One of the attractions was to rent a boat and float down the Deschutes River. Then at a designated area, somebody from the resort appeared, took our boat, and drove us back to our room.

Floating down that river, with song birds and crickets singing their hearts out, was a beautiful time. I think that part of the charm of this was that there was no gasoline or diesel engine to roar and distract from the way that nature sings. We also raced down bicycle paths on rented bicycles.

In Victoria, we stayed at the Empress Hotel, which was the grand old dame, with service and style from the imperial days of the British Empire. Our room was a suite with four windows that overlooked the harbor below. Sometimes birds would fly in and create a commotion. We got dressed up and, as they say, took tea in the dining room. All great fun.

Our next trip as a family was to Washington, DC. Norm Mineta, the congressman to a district close to ours and brother to a coworker of Maie, showed us around the capitol building, He even enticed the quietly observing Alan to sit in the Speaker of the House's chair. Alan was timid, but he looked as if he might someday sit there. He had that little wisp of a smile on his face. I wish I had a picture.

The trip to Palm Springs didn't live up to its expectations. Really, we had three vacations in this place, but somehow it was not quite what we had hoped for. The area was just too big, and the really nice places were off limits to ordinary people.

Next, we ventured farther to Grand Cayman Island. This group of islands is almost in the middle of the Caribbean Sea, far from silt-carrying rivers. Thus, the water is pristine clear and perfectly clean.

We took Maie's parents to this lovely spot, and they remembered it as one of the magical places they never expected to see. The beaches are powdered coral, not the grainy sand of most beaches throughout the world.

A coral reef surrounds the island—actually it is a group of islands with one large one, which is where most people live and visit. This reef protects the shore from the larger waves of open water. So the waves that reach the shore are gentle, just right for someone like myself. It is the kind of beach that Maie likes.

Sylvi and Alan were ready for stronger waves. They found stronger waves in a cove. They also swam with the manta rays. These fish were close to the surface and look like giant shadows, like silhouettes.

We rented a beach house, so we could hear the lapping of the waves all night. That is one of nature's most beautiful sounds.

Next, I planned a trip on the grand scale. It would be the high road to Europe. It would continue for five weeks and carry us through England, Holland, France, Belgium, Switzerland, Germany, Austria, and Italy.

We tried to do too much. That is the sure sign of an amateur traveler.

Our first day in England summed it up. We took a sightseeing bus around London. Five minutes after we sat down, we were all asleep. We saw nothing of London but the bus station.

We went to Oxford and visited my old college, Corpus Christi College. I secretly hoped that somehow the visit might kindle a small flame of inspiration for Sylvi and Alan to attend the college or maybe one of the other colleges of Oxford. That didn't happen. But it wasn't a big disappointment to me. They had their own lives to live, and the choice of college was theirs alone.

While we were at Corpus, Michael Brock, dean of the college and my tutor in British political history, gave us a magnificent luncheon. His wife, Eleanor, prepared cress sandwiches, which are different and more delicious than the usual watercress sandwiches.

We stayed at an old manor house with creaky stairs and a roaring fire in evenings. We went to pubs by the river Isis, which eventually becomes the Thames. In Vienna, there was lots of music, including operas and concerts in gold-lined courts. We saw paintings that were old and some that were blazingly radical. What a feast for the senses!

The manor house in the Cotswalds, near Oxford, was large. It was filled with ancient broken-down furniture. I told Alan he should make a movie here. We were the only guests staying at the house, so we had the whole place to ourselves. We also relaxed. Alan and Sylvi played tennis and watched the trap shootings. We were busy and comfortable.

And so it went, day after day. None of Sylvi's nor Alan's

friends had done anything like this. In the years that followed, some did take similar trips. The trip gave them a vivid sense of Western civilization that no course or lecture could provide. They came home ready to speak up for this deep and rich way of life that we live with every day.

With our travel, we were beginning to reach our own stride. I think we grew closer with the trips.

The next trip was to Japan, and it continued to Southeast Asia. Japan, in particular, was a "must do" trip. Of all of the countries in the world, Japan is the one country that when you arrive, you know that you are really in a foreign land.

For example, when I was changing money, the man next to me described his recent experience. He was still groggy from his airplane ride from the United States and had left his wallet on an open shelf in the airport. He discovered his loss when he was on a train to his hotel. He went back to the place where he believed he had lost it.

A man in an information booth nearby told him to see the police, which he did. They quickly returned his wallet after he identified it. No money was missing. There was never any doubt in his mind that he would retrieve his wallet. "That's the way it is in Japan," he said.

In another example, Sylvi taught English in a private school which was located near Kyoto. She was walking down a pathway on a rainy day. Seemingly from nowhere, an unknown lady ran out of her house, caught up with Sylvi, and held in her hands an open umbrella, ready to keep the rain away. She released the umbrella into Sylvi's hands, and then this good Samaritan scurried away. I think that Sylvi still has the umbrella.

When I dropped my watch on a granite floor in a hotel lobby, the dial and all of the hands fell all over the place. Three staff persons looked horrified and literally dived into the spot. They carefully put the pieces in a completely sealed envelope, so it would be ready for repair. They even referred me to a nearby shop that sold watches and suggested that I might buy an inexpensive watch to tide me over.

Japan is like that. It is a country which has developed the highest standards of ethical behavior. It is a land where personal courtesy has been carried to levels that are not seen elsewhere.

In a way, a trip to Japan is a form of a spiritual journey as much as it is a visit to see the art and products of the land. In fact, I see the products of this country as the embodiment of their spiritually developed ethics and their personal philosophy. It appears strange that such an ethereal base could lead to the development of the world's finest products, including the finest automobiles, finest cameras, finest elevators, to name a few.

When I went through a Toyota automobile assembly line and saw how each worker had the authority—in fact, the responsibility, to stop the line if he or she saw something wrong, I knew that I was watching the reason the people of this remarkable land produce such world-class products. It starts with a state of mind.

We went on to Beijing and found ourselves in another imperial city. These cities always have very broad streets, in order to accommodate thousands of troops marching in formation and hundreds of clanky tanks and trucks. When we saw the city, there were no parades. It was 1987. There were dusty streets with a few grimy taxi cabs. Our hotel was run by Swiss people, and a fence kept the ordinary people out. So much for the worker's paradise.

I was struck by the number of navigational instruments in a home-spun museum. These instruments had been imported from Arab countries in the eighth and ninth centuries. This was a period of flourishing trade in East Asia and the Indian Ocean, when Europe was a backwater collection of primitive farms.

Hong Kong was as vibrant as ever. It serves as a tribute to the power of personal incentives. Virtually everyone in Hong Kong had been poor and, with very low tax rates, had created wealth out of this rocky, barren land. It is the most inspiring city to an economist of the twentieth century. These thoughts occurred to me as we sat around a pool on the thirtieth floor of the Hilton Hotel. It has been an amazing accomplishment.

How wonderful for Sylvi and Alan to see this range of human experience while they were young. We sometimes took along a friend of Sylvi or Alan. They always enriched our travel.

Our next trip returned us to Europe, and then there was another trip to Japan and Thailand.

Then came the trip to Spain and Portugal. We made a great circle around the Iberian peninsula, with a stop in Madrid.

We started in Lisbon. Despite being the most advanced country in the world in navigation during the sixteenth century and possessing an empire of trading cities throughout the seas to the east, west, and south, the country is no longer rich. It retains no benefit from these earlier possessions and trading accomplishments. Great wealth once went through hands here, but none remains.

When we began, the weather was cool. We wore sweaters during the day. So when we rented our car, it seemed to me that we did not need an air conditioner—a wrong decision which we would soon learn.

Passing across northern Spain and down to the Spanish court of the sixteenth and seventeenth centuries set us up for one of the great contrasts in the world. Here, in a rocky desert as far as the eye can see, are buildings and churches decorated in gold, which was robbed from Indians thousands of miles over one or more great oceans. And there was nothing to support this, no businesses or shops or trades people, except an army and navy that bankrupt the country.

Yet as the final word, the artists prevailed. The art is magnificent. There is gold everywhere, and it is set out in spectacular lighting from candles and a few but perfectly placed windows. So poor and so rich.

We felt little of these thoughts at the time, because our non-air-conditioned car was a very hot car indeed.

We also made the huge mistake of filling the fuel tank of the car with fuel oil, which goes by the name of *gaseolo* in Spain. Cleaning the engine of this wrong type of fuel and hoping that the car would then start after all the fuel had been drained took four hours. The car did start—hooray!—and we continued on our hot journey. I should add that we left a trail of black smoke for many miles.

We passed by La Mancha, which is incredibly hot in the summer, as well as the land of Don Quixote. Maie wanted to see this area, but the car was full of sleeping, tired, and heated travelers. I promised Maie that we would make this our destination on our next trip through this country. I hope that I can keep this promise.

The high point of the trip, and one of the highest points of all our trips, was the Alhambra in the south of Spain. We stayed in the Moorish complex and could walk by the pools and gardens in the day and at night, which is the way that they were intended to be seen and experienced. All of this with night stars gleaming overhead.

This place is a gem. It will always cast its magic spell of beauty on all who make their way down its paths and visit its sparkling rooms filled with brilliant hues and gold.

We did not realize at the time that this would be the last of our journeys with the four of us. It has made the memory of the Alhambra all the more precious. We would not feel the closeness and joy of our close family until Sylvi's family with Matthias would take us to Tuscany nearly two decades later. Alan's loss did not go away even then. But there were new voices—those of Noora and Siena—our grandchildren—who opened the heart to new life.

Actually, there was one more trip for the six of us. That

included Ema and Isa. It was the trip to Estonia, and this trip was really a special time for Ema and Isa, so they could return to Estonia.

It was a homecoming. Isa walked down his old paths and showed us the tree branch where he left Ema, much to Ema's surprise. And all of the relatives—they welcomed Ema and Isa as long-lost family.

We were able to make this trip because Estonia had become a separate, free nation, and was no longer under the rule of the Soviets in Russia. Few of us believed this would ever happen in our lifetimes. How wonderful it did happen when it did, with time for Ema and Isa to return.

We have enjoyed visits to Matthias's parents, Maria and Fridolin, in Lucerne, Switzerland. They entertained us in their Alpenhaus on the slopes of a mountain side. It was there that special baptism services were held for Noora. That trip was one with a special purpose.

Maria and Fridolin also asked us to be guests in their home, which we thoroughly enjoyed. They live close to the western shore of Lake Lucerne, whose waters are crystal clear and whose vintage steamers ply the water without leaking a drop of oil.

Chapter 21
Jefferies & Co.
1980 to 2004

Jefferies & Co., Inc. changed my life. It also changed the way that our family lived. Boyd Jefferies and Frank Baxter, as well as others, made huge contributions to my work. They gave me the platform to the securities market.

In addition, they elevated me to the highest ranks of the corporate world. They also rewarded me. I had not anticipated anything like this at all.

It began very modestly. In fact, it began almost in desperation. I was trying to sell subscriptions to my report on the bond market, the *Money Analyst*, and had placed an advertisement in Barron's magazine for a trial subscription. I received thirty-two requests, none of which resulted in an actual subscription.

But the thirty-third request was not a subscription form, but a telephone call from someone I had never heard of—Joe Chiappetta. He wanted to represent me in the New York area. Joe seemed to be sincerely interested in doing this, so I invited him to visit me in California and learn more about the thinking that underpinned the report. He did this. We got along fine, and he returned to New York.

Nothing happened for three weeks. Then Joe started talking about working for Jefferies & Co., which was then a very small brokerage firm headquartered in Los Angeles. I felt that the whole deal had collapsed. But Joe told me to hold on, that Boyd Jefferies might want to use the *Money Analyst* in some way. I was doubtful of this, but at that moment, there were no other alternatives.

Joe turned out to be correct. Boyd wanted a subscription, but what he really wanted was for Joe to take me to potential clients and thus introduce Jefferies to stock traders. I was to be the door opener. This would be the way that his firm would introduce itself to the New York area. The firm had very little business in this territory at the time, and of course, the New York market is the world's largest area for securities trading. This would be a big task, since this firm with sixty-five employees was small by comparison to New York standards.

To check me out, he sent Chuck Matthewson to visit me. Chuck was the ultimate authority of the firm, since he and his friends provided the lion's share of the original investment that got Jefferies started. Chuck is an easy person to talk to and also one of the sharpest businessmen in America. He is legendary in the way he has started numerous businesses that have proven to be remarkably successful.

When he called, I knew it was important. I invited him to

the bank, originally for lunch, which he politely declined, then for an office visit, which he accepted. At the time, my desk was in the middle of a bay of desks, and there was no place for a meeting. So I reserved a conference room, took some papers and put them on the table, put the telephone on the table, and made myself the strangest-looking office you have ever seen. But it was private, and I was ready for Chuck.

We had a great conversation about the market and business. We never talked about Jefferies. He did remark that he had never seen an office like this. I smiled and never said a word.

When the time came for him to leave, which I allowed him to announce, I walked him to the elevator, accompanied him to the street, hailed a cab for him, helped him into the cab, and waved goodbye. It was exactly the intense personal service that I had received from Morgan Stanley several years earlier. It is what I call the Morgan Stanley treatment. I must have passed the test. This was perhaps the most important interview I ever had. In any event, Chuck has become a good friend over the years.

As a trial run, I made calls in New York, as well as in Los Angeles, Chicago, Atlanta, and Dallas. These were small offices of a handful of people. All of the calls went well, and I was invited to the firm's annual get-together in Phoenix. Ron Alghini, the president of the firm, offered me a position. I told Ron I wanted to be associated with the firm, but as a consultant, not as an employee. I had a hunch that would be the way to work together.

Ron didn't care how we would be associated, and he agreed to my proposal. My retainer was set at my salary with Bank of America. But of course, anyone looking at this arrangement would consider the employment with the world's largest bank to be more secure and more valuable than working for a little-known brokerage firm.

But to me, security was less important than opportunity.

I walked out of that meeting feeling on top of the world. Everything was on a small scale, but I would be able to run my own show. Moreover, the enthusiasm and support of the firm at that moment was almost intoxicating. Joe Chiappetta had delivered much more than I ever could have expected.

The arrangement called for one week per month of travel, and I would be free for the rest of the month to write the *Money Analyst*. That meant that I would also be home to be with Maie, Sylvi, and Alan. It meant that I could be an American Youth Soccer Organization (AYSO) coach, go to local community events, and simply be present in the home.

As attractive as this sounded, I still had lingering doubts— what had I forgotten or overlooked? So I talked with Jim Maletis, who had always given me excellent advice since our days together at Shuman Agnew. Jim said, "Take it. It'll be a piece of cake. You will come out ahead." That clinched it.

As it turned out, this arrangement continued for the remainder of my working career, almost one-quarter of a century. It was a gift from heaven.

During the first two years of making calls on customers, I

was teamed up with Reed Bingham, director of marketing for the firm. Reed had the right skills of a door opener. He had just the right amount of push to attract interest on the part of a potential customer. We made calls on virtually all of the largest institutional accounts of the time. Jerry Dayton did the same thing with me on the West Coast. His approach was different, but he was just as successful. He emphasized courtesy. He was always a gentleman and a pleasure to work with.

Boyd was very pleased. He had wanted to enter this upper strata for some time, and now it was happening.

Then Boyd invited me to join the board of directors of the firm. I had been with them for a little more than a year at the time.

Boyd seemed to like what I said, so when he decided to go public with stock of the company, he invited me once again to join this new board of Jefferies Group, Inc. Then this board made me chairman of the compensation committee and chairman of the audit committee, which were the two most central committees of the firm's management.

All the while this was going on, I was making calls in new territories. We gave special attention to New York and opened a branch there. A few days after we opened, Frank Baxter, who was then the new office manager, and I were looking at the half of a floor of empty space, and Frank worried about its extra cost. I turned to Frank and told him not to worry, that within a year he would have filled out every inch of space, and he would be looking for space twice this size. He looked puzzled, but I was right. Frank knew this also. Jefferies offered a superior type of service, and I could see how, for a number of years, it would expand as fast as people could be trained.

Then we gave special attention to London and opened a branch there. Frank Palamara and I made the calls, sometimes as simple as knocking on doors. After that, we did the same in Hong Kong.

The firm grew rapidly. The original spirit of the firm was largely retained. This spirit was both fiercely individualistic and at the same time highly cooperative. Each person was expected to do the best work possible, from the mundane job of picking up the telephone on its first ring to the sophisticated work of making sure each customer's needs were met before being asked. Yet when an account salesperson got into trouble, everyone ran to the rescue and helped out immediately. It was a wonderful sight to behold.

Sometimes we tried to move too fast and forgot things on the way. One of these times, Andy Hall and I were traveling from Abu Dhabi, United Arab Emirates, to Singapore, and when we arrived at the ticket counter in Dubai, I discovered that I had left my passport in my hotel in Abu Dhabi.

Andy didn't flinch an eye but went to a phone, called the hotel, which put the passport into a taxi cab which drove to our airport. I was distressed as I thought of all of the troubles along the way that could happen to that passport. But Andy knew his territory, and he reassured me that the taxi driver in this part of the world would be highly reliable. He was right. One hour later, my passport arrived, right on schedule.

Health is one of the risks that are usually overlooked in traveling to distant places. It caught up with me.

I was leaving Riyadh, Saudi Arabia, and it was one of those desert heat waves that can be appreciated only with experience. I was walking to the departure gate and saw a shiny, new Westinghouse water cooler. I drank heartily. Later, the next day, I didn't feel well. For three weeks, I had indigestion that kept getting worse. Finally, I went to the Palo Alto Medical Clinic and was diagnosed as having *girardia*, a parasite that was common to primitive countries without water purification. The Westinghouse water cooler may have been new, but the water was contaminated from old wells. After a brief treatment, I was well.

How strange it is the way things happen. This ailment kept me from traveling to Florida to attend the funeral of my mother's sister, my aunt Jean. But I was well enough to attend the showing of Alan's latest film at the California College of the Arts. This was his moment of recognition, and I was so pleased to see him appreciated so warmly by everybody at the showing.

It was an auspicious moment in another way, since it was next to the last time I saw him. Two weeks later, he was killed in a car crash. If I had not had that illness from Saudi Arabia, I would now not have that beautiful memory of him. It made me realize that we must never regard anything as unfortunate. It may be what becomes a sublime blessing when all is said and done.

During the period, I was selected by the *Wall Street Journal* to be one of the fifty-four leading economists of the United States and, on two occasions, ranked first in their semiannual outlook survey.

Meetings with customers usually followed a well-traveled pattern. Usually, I outlined what I expected was going to happen to markets in the coming year and a half. This was based on the economic underpinning and the political trends that were likely to be fulfilled over the course of that period.

Then the customers would ask questions. There would sometimes be only one customer, but usually there were three or four. Sometimes there would be twenty-five, as was the case regularly in the State of Texas in Austin.

There is a bit of art to making a presentation. You want to give the story as you see it. But you don't want to be offensive. So sometimes you have to walk a thin line to be informative but also understanding of the customers' points of view. The way I look at success in meetings is whether or not the customer learned something useful and whether we both made a closer friendship. In almost all meetings, I felt that we succeeded. There is no satisfaction greater in business than to walk out of a meeting with that accomplishment.

Sometimes there are surprises. The week of the 9/11 event began uneventfully in Oklahoma, and we were at a breakfast meeting in Oklahoma City when someone burst into the meeting and said that a plane had flown into the World Trade Center. Scott Gooch and Dave Zimansky from the Dallas office were with me.

We passed off the news without much comment, and I went on with my presentation. Then two minutes later someone else bolted in, obviously excited, and said this was a big event. So we all went out to see the television which described in vivid detail the awful events that were taking place.

I stood before the screen and tried to understand what was happening. Then I began to think of our personal situation in Oklahoma City. I knew the planes would be cancelled, and I knew that we were in a place that would not receive much attention. We were stuck where we were. So I went to a phone and called Hertz car rental and asked for the biggest car they had. Fortunately, a Lincoln Town Car was available, and I reserved it for us. Within half of an hour, there were no cars, not even little ones, for rent.

Our schedule called for meetings in Dallas, Austin, and Houston. With Scott as our driver, we would drive to those locations. And what a good driver he was. He cruised at speeds that seemed to rival the airplanes that weren't flying, and I sometimes wondered what would happen if a tire came off. But not to worry. We were in Texas. We made every call on schedule, except one.

Then after everybody said goodbye, came the second test. That was how to get from Houston to San Francisco, which is the airport near my home. It turned out that there was one Continental Airlines flight on Saturday morning that left Houston at seven o'clock. I checked out of my hotel at one o'clock and took a taxi to the airport. With the ultratight security, I made it to the door of the plane with just ten minutes to spare. Many people spent a week in Houston.

Another trip also had its surprise. I was driving alone from Winston Salem, North Carolina to Raleigh. I was to meet E. T. Laird, who was the manager of the Atlanta office, and McKee Nunnally. I was driving comfortably when an irresistible urge came over me to check my seatbelt. I felt that this was strange, but I checked it, and it was fastened. No, this urge demanded that I open and close it to be sure it was locked. I did that and settled back into my seat.

Thirty seconds later, a large semitruck passed me at seventy miles per hour and swayed. The truck's front tire rim bolts caught my front tire and threw my car in front of it. The impact then threw me into the median grass, and I came to rest facing the oncoming traffic but still in the median. The next thing I knew a state trooper was trying to open my door. He asked if I was all right. My only damage was a few cuts on my hand from the shattered glass.

I got out of the car and looked at it. There was a complete wreck. My next thought was whether I was still alive. I couldn't believe what had happened.

The police officer said a witness was sure that I had not survived. It was that bad. After we arranged for Hertz to pick up the car, the police officer offered to take me to Raleigh. And so I arrived at the luncheon appointment for dessert. Of course E. T. and McKee were upset with me. But I didn't explain a thing and gave a few brief remarks. Apparently, the state treasurer was in attendance. That didn't matter. I was alive, and at that moment, that was all that counted.

We went to Hertz so I could get another car. There was my wreck. The boys couldn't believe their eyes.

I asked the greater power why I was spared. There was no answer. But I had to have had help.

There were several efforts from within the board of directors to take over leadership of the company. All were originated by Ron Alghini, who, from the point of view of sheer brainpower, was the smartest person in the company. He demonstrated this very soon after each new member of the board was seated. Ron had the title of president and was the number two man following Boyd.

He could intimidate even the most powerful. All of the members of the board were respectful of his power. His mind kept the board in line for several years. Sometimes this required a battle to show he still had his strength. There were two particularly severe battles, one with Ben Lubin and another with Ray Killian.

The immediate issues were always small. As usual, Ron was completely prepared. Ben challenged Ron, but Ron carefully chose his turf and was in greater command of information.

I never crossed swords with Ron. There was never an occasion for this to happen. I always respected Ron, and I felt his excursions of power could be safely directed toward humbling competitors. In short, I felt we should let him loose on our less skilled competition, and Boyd could ultimately control him if matters got too hectic.

Ron's growing presence on the board led him to make plans to change the headquarters of the firm from Los Angeles to Chicago, where he was located. He planned to move the entire accounting department, which would, in effect, then report to him.

Boyd did not like this, and his response was to hire Ray Killian, who was manager of the Boston office of Goldman Sachs. Ray was brought in ostensibly to be national sales manager, but his real job was to stop Ron from carrying out his plans to consolidate control in Chicago. That led to a bruising challenge.

The outcome was a papered-over truce by all parties, and several months later, Ron resigned his corporate role. At this point, when Boyd was in hot water with regulators, Frank Baxter became president. Frank was the managing director when Boyd was forced to step down due to the government inquiry into the firm's activities.

Boyd was charged with parking stock. This is a practice of retaining stock in the firm's books as an accommodation to a customer. The amount involved was quite small, a little more than one hundred thousand dollars. This performance by Boyd was challenged by the regulators.

During this difficult period, I regarded my role as one which would protect the integrity of the financial reports of the firm through my reputation and representation as chairman of the board's audit committee. I believe that this was successful because of the outstanding work of Maxine Syrjamaki, the firm's chief financial officer. Maxine is the exceptional epitome of what a financial officer should be. Due to her good work, I was not challenged with any report.

At the time the judge was to give his verdict, I flew back to New York City from Munich and arranged a gathering to be with Boyd, so he would be surrounded with friends. That would be important to Boyd, who had gone through terrible moments, days and months. I wanted him to know he had friends regardless of the judge's pronouncements.

The regulators prevailed. Boyd was ordered to pay a fine and perform community service, and he was excluded from trading in the future.

The verdict was much less severe than it might have been, and as the judge read it, there was an easing in the atmosphere of the court, which all Boyd's friends and family felt. I am sure Boyd felt it also, but I never asked him about it.

When we went to our designated private room in a nearby hotel, there was a great outcry for champagne. Since I rented the room, I controlled the refreshments, and I absolutely prohibited any champagne in the room. I didn't want the next day's newspapers to headline, "Ex-Trader Gets Light Sentence and Greets Champagne Reception." This didn't happen, and within an hour, the room was vacant. All was well.

I never felt that Boyd had done anything of major negative importance. Rather, he was the target of several major brokerage firms so that they could clear the way of what Jefferies was doing and have the field open to them. This was particularly the case with high-yield bonds. Regulators are not supposed to act in this manner. But in this case, I think that they did. That is the way it is. In any business that involves public regulators, you have to be squeaky clean beyond reason.

Throughout this entire period, Dorothy Grace, the ongoing executive secretary, kept her cool and provided an important task of maintaining stability and good manners. She rose to the occasion beautifully.

When the dust settled, the firm was intact, although bruised.

Thus ended an era. Boyd was the most original, creative person I ever met in the securities business. He always found a way to get something done, regardless of the impediments in the way. In fact, what hurt him was actively practiced by Wall Street. If there was an infraction, the usual practice of regulators was to send a man around to give a talking to the offender or to send an almost routine letter of noncompliance.

He was generous beyond all comparison. He rewarded good work, and he always spoke highly of work that was effective and well done.

He was a good man, and it was a privilege to count him as a friend. A good and faithful friend.

There is a picture of him in my mind that will always remain. We had assembled for the Jefferies Scholarship meetings for the year. The venue was Banff and Lake Louise, and we had finished our day's work. Boyd, Maie, and I were walking toward the lake when Boyd suggested that we take a canoe out on the lake. Maie bowed out, and I said okay. The truth of the matter was that I was scared to death that we would tumble over and spill into the water, which was icy cold. Then matters turned worse, as I asked Boyd if he would like to take the stern paddle. I did this as a courtesy, but more so as a way of getting him to the position that controlled the boat. He declined, so there I was, paddling and steering. We got under way smoothly. How did I ever do this? We went up close to the glacier at the end of the lake. We remained there for a long time, gazing at this magnificent creation of nature. Then Boyd said, "Let's go back." For some reason, I was able to turn the boat around, quite smoothly as a matter of fact, and return the boat to the dock. We stepped on dry land without incident. Boyd must have thought I was a master boatman. I shall always remember his sitting before me on that fragile boat before an awesome glacier.

As a remembrance of his son Stephen, who died in a motorcycle accident, Boyd established the Jefferies Scholarship Program for the young people of the firm to get a better education. Both Sylvi and Alan received these scholarships, and they meant a lot to both of our children.

The financial support was very helpful, but the recognition was almost more important. That is what I found when I spoke with winners over the years.

I helped wherever I could do so. In one instance, there was a shortage of applicants. So with Alan's help, I designed and filmed a DVD which interviewed applicants, showing what the scholarship meant to them. It proved to be successful, and applications soon picked up.

What a way to be remembered by the firm. Boyd always did things right.

Frank brought peace. He brought integrity. The issues with Boyd had been settled favorably. All of the energy of the firm now went into the business.

With Frank, everything had to be just as it was supposed to be. In one instance, I saw him call for an audit of the bills and expenses of one of the firm's highest officers, and he did this as a matter of procedure. No firm on the street was more responsible. Even so, occasionally there were slips, when the self-imposed position limits on stocks were exceeded. This was rare and, in the enthusiasm for business, can occur as a matter of course.

But the firm's position limits were conservative in the first place, and I never worried about the matter. Still, I insisted that the limits should be used as guideposts for maximum holdings and, when exceeded, should be quickly brought into line. This always happened, and there were no complaints.

Frank brought diversification. He changed the company from being a single product line of stock trading to a more, broadly based firm conducting business in many lines. High-yield bonds were the first of the new business lines. It took three attempts to get this business on its feet. But Frank didn't give up.

Of course, this program of diversification was not without costs. The financial cost was that earnings were not as strong as they would have been, if only the main line of trading business had been the full extent of the company.

Eventually, diversification paid off, and earnings rose more rapidly than the investment community expected. That gave a major boost to the price of the stock. It also meant that stock options would be really worth something. There had been a period when there were serious doubts about the options.

During this period, there was only one instance when I felt Frank was going down the wrong road. He had originally wanted to spin off the division called Investment Technology Group. This business used electronic techniques to automatically buy and sell stock according to formulas that had been predetermined. A major advantage of this type of trading is that everything is set up during quiet times, and a rush of the market has little effect on decisions.

I agreed with this and believed that the Investment Technology Group should be divested from Jefferies. In fact, I rallied for the cause. I based my support on considerable research that showed that companies with complex business lines were worth less to investors than companies with simple lines. Complex companies are difficult to analyze and value. The extra benefit of simplicity is reflected in a higher stock price.

Then for reasons I never understood, Frank changed his mind and decided he didn't want to spin off the Investment Technology Group. So we were at different points when it came to the time to vote. Frank prevailed. Subsequently, Frank changed his mind again and proposed his original position of divestiture. I supported him, as I had originally. The Investment Technology Group was finally set up as a separate company, and it prospered to a far greater extent than it would have had if it had remained within the Jefferies fold.

In all of this, I did what I felt was right for the shareholders and employees. In the end, my view did prevail, and all who were involved prospered. Business is life, and sometimes there are knocks that just have to be shrugged off.

Frank particularly was helpful to me personally. He was always urging me to try new approaches and particularly to take equity analysis under my wing. Until Frank, I had been mainly concerned with bonds and interest rates. He encouraged me to make my work broader and more useful to customers.

I was over seventy years when I retired from the firm. It was a long run, twenty-four years, and a good one. I am grateful for each minute that I was in the saddle.

It was during this period that my mother died. She had undergone an operation for cancer. After that, she refused to eat. I believe this is what her sister, my aunt Jean, did in her final time. Whatever I did had no effect. She had apparently decided to end her days. I felt that I should have done something more. But she ended her days peacefully. I miss her. She had a get-up-and-go spirit that will always be an inspiration to me. I wish I had her last year to live over again.

We wanted her final services to be moving yet simple, as she would have wanted them to be. In this endeavor, Ken and Joyce Kaufman were extremely helpful. Ken organized the service, which we held in a room at her residence. Joyce gave us her quiet assurance and radiated confidence to all who came. I shall always be grateful to these wonderful friends, whose friendship has grown over the years. It is moments like these that show who is close.

My father died due to a weak heart. He had been living in a private home and was looked after by kind people who also lived in that home. In his final years, he was looked after by his second son, Guilford, who is my half brother.

On several occasions, when I had visited him, he approached me and asked that I get him out of his present circumstances. I didn't know what to say. He had mentally slipped but could carry on a clear and coherent conversation. I told him I would help and felt terrible after I said it, because there was nothing I could really do. Toward the end, he had slipped so much that he couldn't live on his own.

Guilf was the ideal person to oversee his care, which involved considerable self-sacrifice. He completely was there for our dad. They both lived in Dayton, Ohio, and my visits were always a high for me to see him and his family and my dad.

When I was traveling, I would stop to see my dad and Guilf and his family; I was warmly greeted, and the days we spent together covered sports in the driveway to the presidential planes in the Dayton Airforce base.

Lori, Guilf's wife, is an inspiring and encouraging mother,

who makes sure her children have the best. And the results show. Corinn is a scholar, a truly excellent scholar. Jack is a sportsman and has a vibrant and energetic personality. He will someday be a very successful businessman. Jesse makes electricity dance. He gets such great pleasure from electronics that I know that he will invent something important.

And it is always a great pleasure to see Guilf. I no longer am traveling, so the occasion for my visits now must be specially focused. This part of my family is a treasure that I don't want to let slip.

Finally, when my dad's heart gave way, an era in my life ended. I am thankful for his being my father and the many ways that he had helped me. He was always generous to me, and he sent me on my way the right way. I am very grateful to him. I also wish that I had his final year to live over.

Chapter 22
Clubs
1960 to 2012

I have not been a joiner of clubs and organizations. But over the years, I have been a member of several groups.

For many years, I was an active member of the Columbia Club of Cleveland and also the Columbia Club of San Francisco. In fact, I was president of the Columbia Club of San Francisco for two years early in my career. I followed Siggy Kempner, the legendary Columbian of San Francisco. I did my duty in fundraising efforts for the people in New York. I was also a so-called official of the Oxford—Cambridge Boat Race dinners, which was a social event of some notoriety.

But I never carried on as did some friends who were real club people. I lived in Palo Alto, which was out of the way for San Francisco–based activities. More importantly, raising two children in Palo Alto was my primary focus.

The most exclusive group that I am a part of, and Maie is with me, is the annual reunion with my two first cousins and their spouses, John and Teresa Weedon and Tom and Judy Bowen.

We get together for a week at some interesting place and take the time to settle the problems of the world and listen to each other. This week is the high point of the year for me.

Nevertheless, in later years, there were four organizations that I gave special attention.

The first was the Committee for Monetary Research & Education, which is headed by Elizabeth Bricker Currier. Actually, my interest began when I was with Bank of America. They are a free and open organization that, from my point of view, happens to be right about issues involving money.

Then a number of years ago, in some way I never quite understood, I became a director of the organization. After the untimely death of Bill Easman, the board voted me to be his replacement as treasurer. This is not an onerous task, as best as I can determine, since the books of the organization are not complicated and balances show little change from year to year.

The group is held together and lives by the wit, insight, and craft of Elizabeth Currrier. She is a remarkable woman in that elevated world of ranked financial and social circles. She fits in everywhere, on the ranch and in society circles.

But most importantly, she has a mission of promoting the integrity of money of the United States. Nothing excites her more than transgressions against this money—and there are plenty of instances of this.

Elizabeth was the first in my world to point out that nothing works in economics without good money. This is simply money that has buying power which stays the same over time. It is a simple rule. But disastrous things happen—not right away, but eventually—when it is not followed.

In modern life, Elizabeth saw this first. And she opened the speakers' platform to all who cared to promote the good money precept.

There are twice-yearly dinner meetings with lecturers who provide the platform. In fact, the speakers provide a heavy amount of information, and by nine o'clock, many attendees wilt under the information they receive.

One of my tasks is to talk with participants and to keep the flame of the organization alive. It is a task of dedication, and these are outstanding people on the board, including the chairman, the Hon. William Middendorf, who has a distinguished career in government, and Walker Todd, who is an old-school scholar—the kind of expert who truly knows his material. An up and coming board member is Daniel Oliver.

The second organization is the Palo Alto Club. This group has a membership of about 175 men who live primarily in the Palo Alto environs. Women do not become members, although once a year, there is usually a dinner that includes wives or significant-other ladies for those who do not have wives.

The club provides lunches during weekdays and has speakers twice a month who discuss a variety of subjects. The speakers are usually those with a national reputation.

All of this takes place in a comfortable residence in the old part of Palo Alto.

The strength of the club is its members and the friendships that evolve largely at the lunches. The banter around the tables is high spirited, and the humorous side of any issue is highly admired. The dinners carry this fellowship further. There are no depressing ends in public to any story, no matter how hopeless it might appear to be.

Nevertheless, I believe that the good-natured feelings cover a deeper concern about life. Underneath it all is the attitude that you have to work with what you have, but if you dig deeply enough, something good will show up.

I like that spirit, and over the years, I have felt that this attitude is a winning one and that it is a resilient way to live. I know several people who begin any discussion with a negative point of view and whose first response is a predictable no. What a depressing way to live.

The leaders in the club know how to put this optimistic spirit into practice. One of these persons, Kent Kaiser, always has a ready hand to help. Another is Bill Reller, who knows the best way to do anything. I should mention Bill Bocook, who whose sage advice always helps. Then there is the sublime humor of Lenard Ware. And not to forget Bill Phillips, who with good fellowship always gets a conversation going. The list goes on.

I joined the club just before I retired from Jefferies. That was a smart move. But I should have joined earlier. That would have been a smarter move.

A third group that has been important to me in recent years is the First Wednesday Club. It is named after its meeting date, which is held on the first Wednesday each month. The club was started by the inspiration of Stan Lachman, who was its leader. John Ray provided a special buoyant fellowship.

The club is comprised of only investment managers who work for a fee, and not sales commissions. These advisors are mostly the traditional investment advisors that we have known throughout our lifetime.

The distinction is considered to be important, because the traditional investment advisor has an incentive to make assets grow, because that advisor is paid on the basis of the size of the assets under management. Commissions from trading carry an incentive for trading, whether or not assets grow. Nevertheless, in fact, both kinds of advisors aim to make assets grow.

In any event, the distinction is important to this group. I do not fit into this description of investment advisor, since I do not manage anyone's assets. I became a member of the group years earlier, I am happy to note, through the invitation of Jack Leylegian, the legendary head of Dreyfus investments and later head of Bank of America investments.

Jack took me under his wing and sat me down into the group, and I have sat ever since, very honored and privileged. My role in the group has evolved so that I have almost become the resident economist. This is quite probably the premier investment forum in Silicon Valley. Jack's son, George, continues the Leylegian presence of always having facts at hand.

There are twenty-six members of the group, and usually twenty to twenty-four members show up for a meeting. The group continues to flourish through the guidance of Chris Croft, who is chairman, and Gordon Harper, who acts as conscience for the group. As can be surmised, this is a very complex and dynamic organization.

During meetings, the discussion covers the waterfront of investment issues. It is really a free for all. Anything is acceptable, and there are no holds barred. There is lots of laughter, but no finger pointing.

Several times a year, an outside speaker makes a presentation on a subject of general interest, such as regulatory requirements or insurance. A Christmas party includes the spouses and gets as close to a celebration as an investment group can get.

Last year, I presented a stock which I felt would rise significantly. It rose the most, and I received a plaque—really—for being lucky.

Before I describe the fourth organization that I have in mind, which would lie in the future, let me give a bit of background.

I studied piano when I was young, but stopped when I started high school. Recently, I felt that I was at a point in my life where playing the piano would be an inspiring activity.

I decided that I would learn one piece well. I would really know it—it would be committed to memory. I would know all of its ins and outs. Only then would I take on a second piece.

For my first piece, I chose Traumerei by Robert Schumann. The work was not easy for me because I had almost forgotten how to read music and the smoothly flowing finger work did not happen automatically.

I bought a 1908 Steinway Model B Grand which had been reconditioned by Acme, a piano rebuilder in Boston. The piano is a dream to play. It is smooth and delicate, as well as full bodied in tone. It has that unique tone of a grand piano, which is like no other instrument.

I practiced almost every day, and the piece began to sound presentable to my ears.

Then I asked two friends to listen to my playing of the piece. I bungled the performance terribly, making all kinds of mistakes. I practiced further and performed the work once more and made fewer mistakes.

I realized from this that an audience changes the way that one performs and that a performer must have experience in knowing how to conduct oneself before listening ears.

I have found the piano is a wonderful instrument, and playing this instrument is a way of expression that is very fulfilling. I hope to continue and add to my repertoire and play for listeners more frequently.

I have also thought about how all of this might be put together in an organized way. It would give to the community an addition to its heritage.

We would set up a music organization in St. Augustine that Sylvi, Matthias, and several of their friends could be involved with. It would feature performances by local amateur pianists and possibly award scholarships.

We would sell tickets for each of three concerts. The concerts would be held on our property with the piano across from a pool which we expect to build. Until the pool would be built, the piano would be on the patio outside the house. The proceeds from the sale of these tickets would go into a fund for scholarships.

The scholarships would be awarded based on the talent and needs of the student. The students could be of any age and would include adults. There would need to be an active committee of perhaps five persons who would promote the performances and the recitals and award the scholarships. The ultimate intent would be that all who apply for a scholarship and participate in the recitals would receive recognition.

There is so much yet to do.

I should add that we recently set up a fifty-two-inch Sony television with surround sound and subscribed to the rebroadcasts in high definition of the Berlin Philharmonic concerts. The sound and sight are remarkable beyond description and have brought a new dimension to music in our home. Technology keeps making the arts better. It is hard to believe that progress in electronics has come so far.

Chapter 23

The Power of Ideas

1987 to the Present

We go through life living off ideas . . . We never give the matter much thought, so we don't realize the power of our ideas.

Sometimes we cross roads with people whose ideas resonate with our own. Then there are rare times when these ideas go beyond us and affect thousands or even millions of people. These individuals are often political figures, poets, artists, and dreamers.

This brings me to Andrus Ansip. Our paths crossed early in his career. We shared ideas initially during a trip he made to our home when the Soviets still controlled Estonia, which is his native land. This is a small country next to Russia and is the last lamp of the West.

He was fascinated by the way things in the public realm were put together. He was searching to understand what made things work.

He was visiting our home with his wife and family, when

we struck up a conversation on economics and how economics explained how things work in a society. He had only heard about the economics of a command society, which was the Soviet approach.

In Estonia at that time, almost everything was owned by the Soviet Union, but there were little things that slipped between the cracks of this monolithic and gigantic structure. In line with Soviet doctrine, these cracks were mistakes and a burden on everyone. According to Soviet doctrine, they should be eliminated. Yet Andrus found them to be what often enabled work to get done and, most basically, for people to get fed.

I can remember the conversations as clear as day. They took place in our driveway, next to our garage. We talked for hours.

Our families are interrelated. His wife, Anu, and my wife are second cousins. They are part of a large extended family that reaches across the ocean and which we have visited.

At the heart of that conversation was the idea that free choice makes life better. Andrus grasped this point immediately. We explored what this meant, and Andrus couldn't hear enough.

It was as if we were back in the classroom when I taught economics, but much more immediate and intense. Andrus was a star student in this transformed classroom.

We had other discussions, and it was clear that he learned his lessons about free market economics very well. When we saw him later, he asked me very sophisticated questions. One was what happens to the worker who lost his or her job. It takes a leap of faith to believe that they will be hired possibly at a better job. This situation is punishment in the Soviet system, but it can be opportunity in ours.

The conversation went on and on, with each point leading to another avenue of thought.

Andrus had a small business, originally an ice cream shop and then additionally selling pizza. He had been able to import an ice cream mix from Switzerland.

The ice cream was outstanding. He sold it during a hot session of a song fest, where his competition was state-produced ice cream that kept its frozen shape even when it melted and tasted terrible. He sold all he could produce, while the Russian ice cream piled up in a warehouse. What a thought.

Andrus was elected to parliament when Estonia regained its freedom. Then he was voted prime minister, a great honor and responsibility.

Subsequently, I arranged through Sally Herrick of the Hoover Institution—a distant relative by marriage—for Andrus to address this organization. They were enthusiastic, and he delivered one of the finest speeches on government that I have ever heard. George Schultz, who is perhaps the most distinguished elder statesman of the United States, was in the audience, and, when Andrus completed his remarks, sprang to his feet and applauded vigorously.

Andrus is now one of the leading spokesmen of Western civilization. He stands proudly and forcefully as a spokesman for all that we believe to be worthwhile in government and daily living.

Andrus said some kind words about me at this meeting and at other gatherings, which were quite undeserved. It is he alone who deserves the good words. I was merely a passerby at an auspicious moment.

Chapter 24

The Present

The writing of memoirs gives a view of an entire life. The broad scope of one's efforts and decisions can be satisfying, and it can also be unsettling.

I won't try to figure out a conclusion, because the remaining pages have not been lived, and I am sure that there are challenges ahead that I cannot now imagine. Who knows how they will be met.

I begin with a marvelous family that includes my wife, Maie, who has been with me through thick and thin for almost one half of a century. It includes my daughter, Sylvi, and her husband, Matthias, and their two children, Noora Pearl and Siena Jade.

It is the future of our two grandchildren that we especially anticipate the most because so much remains unknown.

But some things I do know.

Noora Pearl

Noora is an artistic young lady. She loves dance and rhythm and can tap her feet to the sound of the most faraway drum. She loves art and drawing especially. I expect that she will develop her skills with color soon.

She is as playful as a kitten and never fails to engage me in all sorts of antics. One of these is to tell me that an alligator is about to eat me up and there is nothing that I can do. I pretend to be scared and ask her to save me. It's all acted out in high spirits, as can happen only with children.

We take rides to the ice cream store. She likes chocolate ice cream, followed by strawberry. She rides her little bicycle which has two training wheels to keep her steady. Sometimes she wants to race with me, but we have to be careful with this, because when her bicycle gets going too fast, it isn't stable. Happily, we haven't had any accidents.

Noora likes to work with her hands. She looks forward to her crafts and daily gains dexterity in this activity. It is wonderful to watch her skills develop.

Siena Jade

Siena follows Noora in activities, and it is still early for me to see what her own personal interests are. She is still under her big sister's shadow. This will likely continue.

Whatever personality she develops will be distinct and forceful. I expect it will be a unique, magnetic personality.

Siena grabs hold of you with her eyes and doesn't let go until she wishes to do so. Her attachment is more than beneficial—it is almost therapeutic. It is as if she has innate talents of wellness and healing.

I expect that this will manifest itself with caring for animals or helping people in the way that they go about their daily lives.

So much remains to be revealed with Noora and Siena. I hope that I will be here to watch it happen.

Noora and Siena are my great hopes. It is their future that I anticipate the most. I can see already that their personalities are vibrant. What a joy it would be to see each of them walk down at least one of life's aisles. Maybe I will be given that privilege. If my good luck holds out, that could happen.

We now have two homes, and we are constructing a third. One home is in Palo Alto, California. This is our long-standing home where we spend most of our time.

The second is at Pine Mountain Lake, in Groveland, California. This is our vacation home, although it could also serve as a permanent home as well.

The third will be in St. Augustine, Florida. It will be located next to Sylvi and Matthias's home. Sylvi and Matthias have encouraged us to build this home. I am grateful to them for this. It will turn out to be a comfortable home, I am sure.

Maie and I don't need all of these residences. One nice home is plenty. But for now, they are lovely places to hang your hat.

Bunny and Claude Rust have been frequent visitors to both

of our California homes. They are always entertaining, and hardly a moment goes by without wit and a good joke.

In looking ahead, there are two important new challenges that will test me all the way.

First, there is the challenge of handling my case of Parkinson's disease. This affliction has been with me for almost ten years, but it has advanced slowly. I am, as a result, not much disabled, if any appreciable amount at all. In fact, many people are surprised to learn that I am a pronounced sufferer.

I believe that my health actually got better in the past two years. I realize that the doctors tell us that this is impossible, but experience is the real test of everything. And my experience has been positive.

Yet Parkinson's is a quixotic malady. It can proceed at one pace for several years and then quite unexpectedly take a new turn. You never know.

I have tried a large number of nonconventional treatments, including four acupuncturists, high amounts of vitamins, and various prescription drugs. And there were electronic wands to mention another approach. Three homeopathic doctors and their remedies had their turns. Twice, I slept seven consecutive nights with magnets over and under my head as powerful as a MRI. We also had a gigantic magnet under our mattress which gave Maie unhappy dreams. Maybe I didn't continue these treatments long enough, but I felt nothing worked.

Or maybe the right answer is just the reverse. Maybe something did work and was responsible for my being in as good condition as I enjoy. Nobody knows, but I am glad that I did all of these things.

I believe that a cure probably lies right under our noses, but we don't know it. One of our contributions to the cause has been to establish a reward of one hundred thousand dollars to the person who discovers a cure. We have set up a screening committee and are hopeful that a cure is found and we can make the award.

I was asked by scientists at Elan Pharmaceuticals if I would address their scientists, workers, and senior management. This company is the largest developer of new drugs for Parkinson's. They asked me to talk about what it means to be a Parkinson's patient. When I showed up, there were one hundred fifty people that overflowed the room, and people were standing in the doorway.

What surprised them the most was my comment that Parkinson's patients are unhappy with the slow progress—if that is the right term—with the development of new and better treatment. There has been an abundance of scientific research which has not lead anywhere in finding a cure. It is as if the people involved have research and technical rewards, but there do not seem to be similar efforts to find a cure and treat actual patients.

I added that this has been the way of all medicine in the past two decades. Parkinson's is only part of this broader picture. The answer has to be new and more powerful incentives for individuals to find a cure.

The second challenge will be to keep writing. The idyllic thing about writing is that it requires so few accoutrements to do the work. In fact, nothing requires less equipment or is more austere in its requirements. A pen and a sheet of paper is all that is needed. If you are fancy, a small computer will do. You can carry this equipment anywhere you please. This holds true for words as well as music.

Yet what quiet or thunderous images of the mind flow from these basic and fragile implements.

I had this demonstrated to me a few weeks ago when Maie said she was going to enter a contest that was promoted by the president of Estonia. The contest was to write about why a person would want to return to Estonia. Apparently, a considerable number of people have emigrated from Estonia, and the government is concerned about this.

Maie wrote her piece. Just for the fun of it, I asked Maie if I could also write something and contribute it. I got the green light and put together a writing which was in free verse poetry. To look at the topic of what it meant to be an Estonian, I based my thought on eight trips to this land, knowing many people for forty years and walking the steps of many whom I had not met but had given their lives for freedom. I also knew the story of the people of the country.

I wanted this writing to touch the hearts of those who would listen and who could hear. Most of all, I wanted to be considered as a part of these generous and sacrificing people.

As I approached the writing, I had a strong feeling that we

would make a trip to someplace special in Estonia during the summer, even though we had other plans. The feeling of our presence in this location was quite vivid, and I told Maie that we should expect an unplanned trip to a magnificent place in Estonia. She paid no attention to these thoughts.

Time passed, and we forgot about the writings. Then in the mail came the announcement that I had been selected to receive recognition at the presidential palace in the summer. At first, Maie was in disbelief. I told her that she should have been selected.

When the dust settled, I showed up at the assigned time, walked up to the secretary of education of Estonia, and received a six-volume dictionary of the Estonian language. I couldn't read one word in these volumes but shook the hand of President Ilves.

I am proud of that little piece of writing. It is an homage to an enduring people who have been trampled on over and over and over yet still muster the courage to rise with a purpose. It brings tears to my eyes when I think about it.

It also shows me—and all who know me—that after many years, I can still stir people's lives. I don't believe that I have reached the end of the line yet. In fact, the best is yet to come. Really, I believe that.

I am grateful to Hartwell Brown, a wonderful friend, who has kept my computer humming. He and his new wife are a delight to behold. Hartwell can make the computer do anything.

Professional History
Tracy Herrick

Associate Economist, The Federal Reserve Bank of Cleveland, 1960 to 1962

Economist, The Federal Reserve Bank of Cleveland, 1962 to 1963

Manager Business Planning, Ferro Corporation, 1963 to 1968

Manager Corporate Planning, Ferro Corporation, 1968 to 1969

Economist, Stanford Research Institute, Intl., 1970 to 1973

Senior Economist, Stanford Research Institute, Intl., 1973

Senior Securities Analyst, Shuman Agnew & Co., Inc., 1973 to 1975

Vice President, Shuman Agnew & Co., Inc., 1975

Senior Financial Consultant, Cashiers Division, Bank of America, 1977 to 1979

Author, Bank Analyst's Handbook, 1977

Vice President, World Banking Division, Bank of America, 1979 to 1980

Author, Timing, 1981

Chief Economist, Jefferies & Co., Inc., 1980 to 2004

Author, Power and Wealth, 1988

Director, Jefferies & Co., 1981 to 2004

Director, Jefferies Group, Inc., 1983 to 2004

Chairman, Compensation Committee, Jefferies Group., Inc., 1983 to 2001

Chairman, Audit Committee, Jefferies Group, Inc., 1983 to 2002

Index

Gott, Richard, 98
Grace, Dorothy, 296
Graff, Henry, 76, 249
Gramma Smith (Tracy's
      grandmother), 15–16,
      62–64, 327
Guilford (Tracy's half brother),
      144, 301–2, 327

H

Hall, Andy, 288
Harris, Lowell, 85
Herrick, Blanche, 2
Herrick, Stanford Avery, 1
Herrick, Tracy Ellis, 3, 335
Herrick, Tracy Grant
      as a member of numerous
            clubs, 303
      Bank Analyst's Handbook, 245,
            264
      being caught riding a bike, 29
      being launched as a securities
            analyst of Shuman
            Agnew, 220
      being promoted, 112
      birth of, 1
      birth of the daughter of, 171
      buying a new house, 210
      capsizing the boat, 35
      dealing with Parkinson's
            disease, 318
      death of the father of, 301

death of the grandfather of,
      117
death of the grandmother of,
      93
death of the mother of, 300
death of the son of, 190
directing the choir, 66
dispute with grandmother
      over religion, 27
divorce of the parents of, 11
going to Beijing with family,
      277
going to California, 69
going to college, 67
going to Disneyland with
      family, 272
going to Estonia with Maie,
      233
going to Europe with family,
      274
going to grammar school, 23
going to Grand Cayman
      Island with family, 274
going to Hong Kong, 247
going to Hong Kong with
      family, 278
going to Japan with family,
      276
going to Oxford, 91
going to Puerto Rico, 120
going to Spain and Portugal
      with family, 278

Author's Background

Tracy Herrick was born and raised in Lakewood, Ohio, where he attended public schools.

This is also a personal book about a father who in his lifetime experienced a number of vivid premonitions, including one that involved the death of his son, Alan, in a tragic automobile accident. The accident subsequently happened and claimed the life of the son.

It is the story of a man who felt the immense suffering of Estonian refugees during the Second Great War, as well as during the Soviet oppression following that war. He was honored by the president of Estonia for his effort to instill freedom to all who could hear.

After a distinguished career in banking and finance, he was recruited by Jefferies & Co. Inc., and soon became chairman of the board of the director's audit and compensation committees. Throughout his twenty-five years with this firm, he visited senior clients and presented unique commentaries on the securities markets, which were highly respected.

He lives with his wife in Palo Alto, California. Their daughter and her family live in St. Augustine, Florida.

Lightning Source UK Ltd.
Milton Keynes UK
UKOW052345170613

212392UK00001B/338/P